1698

BRITISH COLUMBIA
THIS FAVOURED LAND · LIZ BRYAN

DOUGLAS & McINTYRE · VANCOUVER / TORONTO

Half-title photo: The Black Tusk, near Vancouver. Al Harvey

Frontispiece: Douglas-fir and hemlock forest, Vancouver Island, Al Harvey

Opposite page: Skagit Valley, Cascade Range. Fred Chapman, Photo/Graphics

Following page: Long Beach, Vancouver Island. Al Harvey

The watercolor paintings which appear throughout the book are the work of Jack Grundle. They were commissioned expressly for this publication.

Douglas & McIntyre Ltd., 1615 Venables Street, Vancouver, British Columbia

Canadian Cataloguing in Publication Data:

Bryan, Liz

British Columbia, this favoured land

Bibliography: p.
ISBN 0-88894-362-8

1. British Columbia — Description and travel — 1950-* I. Grundle, Jack, 1922- II. Title.

FC3811.B79   917.11   C82-091212-3
F1087.B79

Printed and bound in Canada

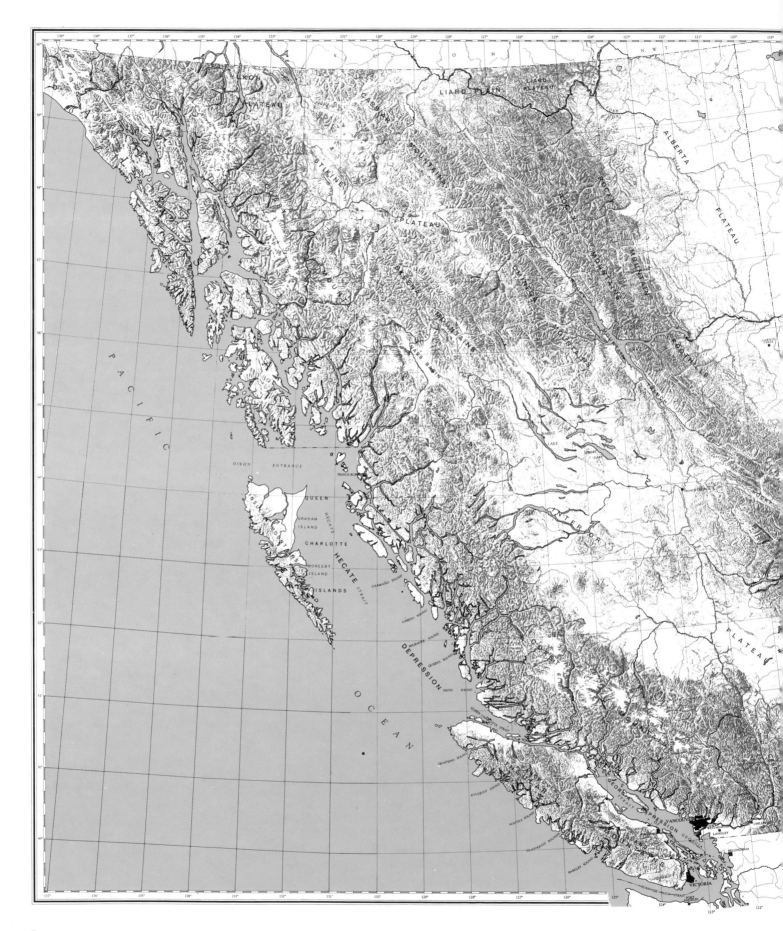

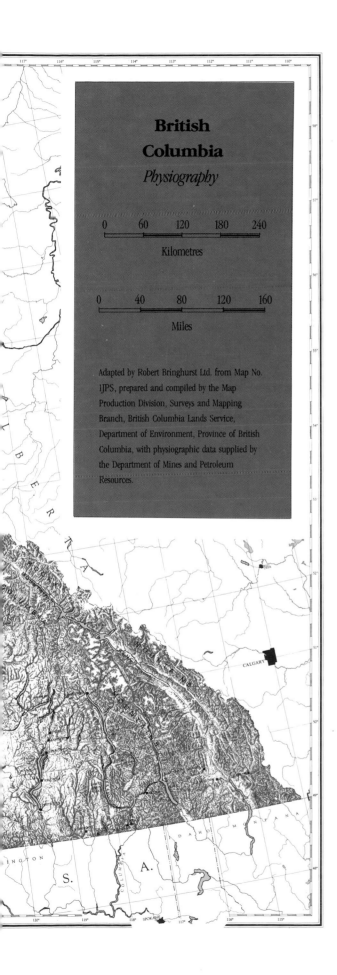

British Columbia

Physiography

0   60   120   180   240

Kilometres

0   40   80   120   160

Miles

Adapted by Robert Bringhurst Ltd. from Map No.
IJPS, prepared and compiled by the Map
Production Division, Surveys and Mapping
Branch, British Columbia Lands Service,
Department of Environment, Province of British
Columbia, with physiographic data supplied by
the Department of Mines and Petroleum
Resources.

Contents

Beach rocks on Murchison Island, Queen Charlotte archipelago. Daniel Conrad

Introduction

Mt. Robson. J.A. Kraulis, Photo/Graphics

*B*ritish Columbia is topographically bewildering: a maze of mountains and rivers, a fractured coastline. Its cold and mountainous terrain was difficult to explore and settle, and much of the province is still mostly uninhabited and uncultivated, though not unmarked by man. In all of its 950 000 square kilometres, there are only 2.7 million people, most of whom are concentrated in the southwest, living an urban life around the balmy lowlands of the Strait of Georgia. Those who live here often find it difficult to comprehend the extent of the huge and lonely land that stretches northwards for 1600 kilometres. Yet even the ingrained city dweller is affected by this vast hinterland, and not only economically, for living on the edge of something bigger and more permanent than ourselves cannot help but change, in some inchoate way, our vision of the world and our place in it.

By far the greatest number of people in British Columbia live in cities and towns. Ten times as many work in manufacturing, trade, commerce and government as in forestry, agriculture, mining and fishing. This contradiction of a dominantly urban society in a province where more than 90 percent of the land is unpeopled wilderness creates a kind of tension, difficult to define but which nevertheless gives life here a keen sense of difference. British Columbians see themselves as unlike other Canadians: less entrapped by materialism, more attuned to the out-of-doors — which is everywhere accessible — more committed to nonurban recreation, and favoured by a land that is still beautiful and still full of promise.

If one were to bisect British Columbia along an east-west axis slightly north of Prince George, the top half of the province — approximately 475 000 square kilometres — would appear as a bleak, boreal land of forest, muskeg and alpine tundra connected to the southern half by two roads and one railway. The few communities are tied to the region's main resources: minerals in the northwest, fossil fuels in the northeast.

A similar but less dramatic trend would emerge if one were to bisect the southern half of the province on an east-west line just north of Kamloops. The northern section comprises the unconfined forested reaches and grassy benchlands of the Cariboo-Chilcotin, the upper Fraser and a vast expanse of mountainous coastline, reached only from the sea. This quarter of the province is also sparsely populated but has better transportation routes to the south.

In the southern quarter of B.C., the series of north-south valleys which encouraged early transportation routes and determined settlement patterns, were historically the most travelled, the earliest to be settled, the fastest to be developed . . . and the first to experience resource depletion. It is here, the warmest, most accessible part of the province, where most of the people live.

The remaining portion of the province is Vancouver Island,

anchored off the southernmost shore. Geographers expect that one day the Lower Mainland will merge economically with southern Vancouver Island, creating one huge integrated megalopolis and engulfing the cities of Victoria, Nanaimo, Vancouver, New Westminster, and all surrounding communities. Until this happens, the island must be considered separately; its 31 000 square kilometres make it comparable in size to the British Isles.

It sustained the first northwest coast settlement and became the first political entity: a separate British colony. Victoria, its headquarters, became the capital of the province in 1868 and from then until the turn of the century it was by far the biggest, richest and most powerful centre in B.C. No longer the largest city, Victoria still holds the political reins. It enjoys a Victorian urbanity preserved in its turn-of-the-century brick and stone architecture, and a theatrical veneer of English charm. The parliament buildings dominate the downtown harbour, and government pay cheques help bolster the city's economy.

To Canadians of other provinces Vancouver Island seems a lotusland. In February snows they dream of island daffodils. They spend their vacations here, year after year, and then come to retire. Perhaps islands by their very nature possess a quality of isolation that appeals to those long trapped inland in one of earth's largest continents. Certainly island weather is balmy, at least on the south and east coasts. (The west coast is sodden, the north both sodden and cold.) Its beautiful maritime and mountain scenery, and the enchanting diversity of the offshore Gulf Islands, provide reasons enough for the area's tourist appeal.

But most visitors to the island are scarcely aware that this is a land still economically dependent on the forest. The main highway stays generally close to the settled southeastern shore, which gives an impression of a pastoral economy. The northern part of the island, with its harsher climate and mountainous terrain, was never settled as extensively as the south. The highway north from Campbell River through Kelsey Bay to Port Hardy on the windy north coast gives a truer picture of the island's nature as it slices through kilometre after kilometre of dank coastal forest. Apart from the east coast road and two roads to the west coast, the island hinterland is inaccessible, and much of it is mountainous wilderness where patches of virgin rain forest still survive.

The Lower Mainland, including the great valley of the Fraser River and the coastal fjords north to Lund, is dominated by Greater Vancouver —home to half the province's population. The city sprawls some 40 kilometres east into Fraser Valley farmland, part way up the slopes of the North Shore mountains and over more than half of the river delta's marshes and wetlands. With a population of 1.5 million, Vancouver is Canada's largest western metropolis and still growing.

Sociologists studying the cumulative effects of generations of city

14

life have begun to question the desirability of huge urban conglomerates — Tokyo, London, New York. Fortunately, Vancouver is still small compared to many other cosmopolitan cities and has physical restraints on future growth that could be its salvation. Hemmed in by sea, mountains, the United States boundary, and the funnel of protected Fraser Valley agricultural lands, Vancouver cannot spread outwards much farther but must plan for increased density. One hopes that urban planners can accommodate the growing population without loss of the quality of life that Vancouver, despite its size, still enjoys. Much of this quality is due to the city's location, within sight and sound of the sea and the uplifting presence of the mountains. Residents may complain that downtown highrises are shouldering out the view of sea and mountains, but the alternative — a city sprawling 150 kilometres from Point Grey to Hope — is surely untenable.

Travelling eastwards from Vancouver, the Trans-Canada Highway slices through the Fraser Valley, the most important agricultural land in the province. The valley depended for a long time on the river for access, and the early settlers cleared plots within reach of steamboat landings. The first wagon road, from New Westminster to Yale, and both transcontinental railways reinforced this riverline character of settlement, though in time the fertility of the land encouraged total pre-emption for agriculture even of the forested glacial uplands, and dyking and drainage brought other areas into production. Today's travellers see a land totally cleared and settled, a patchwork of fields and meadows, dairy farms and berry patches, against a stupendous backdrop of mountains, the Coast Range to the north, the Cascades to the south. No longer a natural environment, the valley's cultivated scenery nevertheless provides solace for the agrarian yearnings that lie not too deeply buried in all of us.

At Hope the mountain ranges converge and the Fraser River squeezes south through the gap between. For thousands, perhaps millions, of years the Fraser has been churning water through this gap, water brown with sediment and debris scoured from B.C.'s heartland. The immense abrasive force of the turbulent river has carved into the adamantine granite of the mountains a deep and sinuous trench which, despite the difficulties of passage, provides the main transportation route between coast and interior. Clinging to the steep canyon sides came the first explorers; crude trails were hacked out, then the first perilous wagon road, two transcontinental railways and finally a modern highway forced their way through. Today, except during spells of winter spite, when the mountains hurl down avalanches, the canyon can be traversed with ease, but it remains a wild and menacingly beautiful place.

When the road emerges from the last long canyon tunnel, it leaves behind the wet coastal climate and embraces the heady air of the dry interior which seems to have a special clarity. In the canyon, as the road

Beach at the foot of Tow Hill, Graham Island, Queen Charlotte archipelago. Ed Gifford, Photo/Graphics

races ahead through Boston Bar and Lytton (where it leaves the Fraser to follow the clear waters of the Thompson River), the forest changes gradually from wet redcedar and hemlock to ponderosa pine and interior fir. Beyond, the dry forest thins out until it is replaced by arid slopes of sagebrush and the irrigated hay meadows of Ashcroft and Cache Creek. Here the Trans-Canada Highway and the railways turn east to thread their ways across the continental divide, but the old wagon road, now Highway 97, continues north through the Cariboo region. All the way to Quesnel, the Cariboo is parkland, alternately grassland and jack pine forest, its rolling meadows stippled with aspens and reedy lakes. The country was explored first by fur traders, but gold in Cariboo creeks opened it up to settlement. Today this land is still mostly ranch country, though forestry and the tourist trade are important too, and mining interests continue to probe for likely prospects.

The Cariboo — always a loosely defined region — comprises the area east of the Fraser's great trench. West of the river lies the Chilcotin, akin to the Cariboo in terrain and land use but increasingly wilder and more forested from east to west. A single, mostly unpaved road heads west from Williams Lake along the roller-coaster of the Fraser Plateau, traverses the Coast Range through Heckman Pass, cuts through the wilderness expanse of Tweedsmuir Provincial Park, then drops precipitously to the Bella Coola River and into the coast rain forest for its final run to the sea. Bella Coola, linked by this solitary road, is an agricultural enclave and a centre for commercial fishing.

North from Williams Lake, Highway 97 leads through almost uninterrupted jack pines to Prince George, 800 kilometres from Vancouver and considered to be the geographical centre of the province. Once the fur traders' Fort George, the city is at an important crossroads: Highways 97 and 16 and two railways, British Columbia Rail and the Canadian National Railway, meet here from the four points of the compass. Prince George, an important centre for forest industries and mining, is probably the fastest growing of all the interior cities. Three large pulp mills are located at this hub.

From Prince George, Highway 16 heads northwest across the central plateau to the Bulkley and Skeena valleys and the sea at Prince Rupert, where a superport for shipment of northern coal, sulphur and potash is planned. Not until 1908 did the first road open up this area to homesteading, and limited arable land and harsh winters have restricted population growth. The area's economy is based principally on the natural resources of forests, minerals and fish, with the aluminum smelter and attendant industries at Kitimat providing additional employment.

The forested coastline south from Prince Rupert all the way to the Lower Mainland — 700 kilometres as the crow flies — is a labyrinth of inlets and islands, nearly all unreachable except by sea. Only a handful of tiny fishing and logging settlements brave the isolation and the battering seas. While civilization has yet to reach the offshore islands and the still heavily glaciated mountains of the mainland coast, logging and mining operations as well as fishing fleets chip away at these no longer boundless resources.

The largest group of northern islands, the Queen Charlottes, are also the farthest flung; their northern edge lies 130 kilometres west of Prince Rupert. In all there are some 150 islands, though most of the land mass is contained in two, Graham and Moresby, and the eastern half of Graham is home to 80 percent of the 5000 population, many of whom are Haida Indians. The islands' mild wet climate has encouraged forests of unbelievable exuberance, and salmon and halibut formerly teemed in the offshore waters. Until fairly recently, the Charlottes were by-passed by "civilizing" man, but inevitably their abundant woodlands have been diminished. Today on South Moresby only a remnant of the original rain forest remains.

Inland from Prince Rupert, the Hazelton area of the Upper Skeena was an important centre for the Tsimshian Indians, and their totem poles still survive as reminders of their rich culture. Some of the finest are at the village of Kitwanga, the takeoff point for one of B.C.'s newest resource roads, punched 800 kilometres through wilderness forest to link with the copper seaport of Stewart, the huge asbestos mines at Cassiar, and to join with the Alaska Highway at the Yukon border. This road, which also connects with the lonely settlement of Telegraph Creek on the wild Stikine River, cuts through vast unpeopled distances of forest, lake and mountain, still nearly pristine in its remoteness.

From the Prince George hub, Highway 97 meanders almost 1600 kilometres northwards to Lower Post on the Yukon border. This north-eastern corner of the province is Peace River country, geologically part of the Canadian plains and the last major region of B.C. to be settled. (Its first homesteaders came from Alberta.) The building of the Alaska Highway from Dawson Creek in 1942 and the connection south to Prince George a decade later provided communications with the south, alleviated isolation, and encouraged settlement on the fertile farmlands of this, the most important grain-growing area of B.C.

The extension of B.C. Rail north to Dawson Creek and later to Fort Nelson further helped integrate the Peace River area with the rest of B.C. Damming of the river for hydro power, the introduction of new forest industries, the discoveries of huge deposits of natural gas and oil, and the building of pipelines to funnel these resources to the power-hungry southwest have changed the character of the region. Mining of extensive coal deposits will change it further. Agricultural emphasis is giving way to industrial activity, and ecological concerns are being raised.

Aspen and fireweed on the Spatsizi Plateau. Fred Chapman, Photo/Graphics

Rabbitbrush, Russian thistle and sage near Big Bar, Fraser Valley. Richard Wright, Photo/Graphics

The populous southeastern regions of the province are most easily reached by Highway 3 which, as it heads east to the Alberta border, reveals the washboard nature of the southern landscape. From Hope the road leaves the Fraser River flatlands and climbs steeply up through the wet coast forests to Allison Pass in the Cascade Mountains. Here a large area of magnificent mountain scenery has been preserved in Manning Park.

Across the divide, in the Similkameen River watershed, the forest zones merge once again, and by the time the road runs out of the mountains, the dry benches above Princeton support sagebrush and ponderosa pine. Princeton is the southernmost outpost of the grasslands which climb north over a plateau to Merritt and on to Kamloops. This is cattle country, physically and economically an extension of the Cariboo, with 2000-metre mountains separating it from the Okanagan to the east. Merritt, in the Nicola Valley, is a sawmill community whose economic base is strengthened by the presence of nearby open-pit copper mines. To the north, Kamloops on the Trans-Canada Highway at the junction of the North and South Thompson rivers was founded as a fur traders' fort in 1813 and has grown into the main marketplace for beef cattle and an important centre for forestry, pulp milling and mining.

East of Princeton, Highway 3 follows the Similkameen River past the old gold town of Hedley through a widening dry-belt valley to Keremeos where the semiarid slopes give way to orchards. The road climbs again over Richter Pass and drops down circuitously into Osoyoos at the southern end of the Okanagan Valley, one of the best fruit-growing areas in all Canada. From Osoyoos over 150 kilometres north to Vernon, this valley is strung with blue lakes bordered by orchards of peach and apricot, cherry, apple and pear, the southern slopes green with vineyards. Earlier, the valley's natural grasslands were ranched to provide beef for the gold miners and later for construction crews of the CPR. In 1892 a railway southwards encouraged more intensive settlement as speculators bought up the land for orchard subdivision. Irrigation was needed, however, before orchards flourished. Today, with much of the best land lost to urban expansion and because of a limited water supply, the agricultural potential of the valley has been curtailed. The area is now heavily dependent on tourism, and a valiant attempt is being made to improve the quality of the lakes for recreational purposes.

North of Vernon, hard frosts make the valley less suitable for fruit, and the land changes to dairy farms before merging into the interior wet belt at Sicamous, on the western edge of Shuswap Lake. The southern expanse of the valley is one of the driest regions in Canada, a semidesert country where cactus and sagebrush flourish. Unfortunately, the irrigation needed to grow fruit destroys the fragile desert environment.

From Osoyoos to the Crowsnest Pass, on the Alberta border,

Highway 3 snakes and climbs to find the easiest route across several mountain ranges. This is Kootenay country, a complicated succession of long, north-south lakes, high peaks and rivers that double back on themselves. The West Kootenay–Boundary area was settled relatively early because of mining discoveries and ease of access via the American railroads. It encompasses the farmlands of the Kettle River–Grand Forks area, the mining, smelting and pulp mill complex at Rossland, Trail and Castlegar, an agricultural pocket of reclaimed land at Creston, and sparsely settled valleys north up Slocan and Kootenay lakes which connect with Revelstoke on the western side of Rogers Pass. This is rugged country, scarred with old mines, but with lake and mountain scenery still beautiful. The East Kootenay, mainly contained by the great valley of the Rocky Mountain Trench, relies on the rich resources of its southern regions — the silver/lead/zinc of Kimberley, the coal of Crowsnest, together with the ubiquitous pulp mills and forest industries. East, Highway 3 climbs through the marred scenery of Crowsnest Pass coalfields into the foothills of Alberta. North of Kimberley on Highway 95 industrial signs fade and the highway along the trench becomes enjoyably scenic as it wends its way past lakes and hot springs and the marshes of the meandering Columbia River to Golden. Connecting roads from Golden lead into Alberta over the Rockies via the Sinclair and Kicking Horse passes and west over Rogers Pass back to Shuswap country.

This, then, is a catalogue of British Columbia's scenic diversity and rich resources. The photographs in this book bear witness to the province's beauty. They were chosen carefully to show the land as it was before man came — a consummate wilderness. It is remarkable that such photographs can still be taken in a province whose people enjoy one of the highest standards of living in the industrialized world, a living derived almost entirely from the exploitation of natural resources.

That B.C. still has much unsullied beauty may reflect the fact that civilizing man and his machinations have only recently been let loose here — or perhaps the land itself is obdurate. In any case, there is still so much worth saving, and British Columbians are now beginning to focus on the problems of the vanishing wilderness and the dangers of uncontrolled development of the land's resources. Books such as this one, which was initiated and encouraged by the B.C. Ministry of the Environment, show that the conservation movement — to guard what is left from profligate use — has increasing government support. And with support, British Columbia, this favoured land, may yet survive for our grandchildren to enjoy.

Paintbrush and salal in the Coast Range. Bob Herger, Photo/Graphics

Algae on basalt, Hippa Island, Queen Charlotte archipelago. Daniel Conrad

Foundations

The Wolves' Ears, Valhalla Range. Pat Morrow, Photo/Graphics

*B*orn in fire, swamped by the sea, heaved skyward and crumpled by the earth's internal tensions, scarred by ice and sluiced by rains, British Columbia today is a land with an astoundingly diverse topography. Its geological story started about four and a half billion years ago when a cloud of gas and primordial dust began to coalesce into the solar system. The molten earth, wrapped in a shawl of dense steam clouds which muffled the sun's heat, slowly began to cool. As the clouds condensed, rain fell. At first this water vaporized instantly on the earth's hot surface, but after thousands of years of ceaseless rainfall and evaporation it stayed to form the first oceans. When the cloud layer thinned to let through filtered sunlight, the essential elements for life were ready.

After two billion years of volcanic eruption, earthquake, flood and fire, deeply buried magma solidified into granite and schist and heaved upwards to form the rocks of the Canadian Shield — among the oldest on earth — the foundation of the North American continent. Where the western mountains now stand, a warm and shallow sea rocked endlessly with the tides, its floor scarred north to south by the curving Cordilleran trough. Into this trough washed rock sediments eroded from the shield by winds and rains and carried by west-flowing streams. As the sediments piled up, the floor of the trough sank, a process that continued for the next 400 million years. It was during this time that life began in the seas. One of the most extensive fossil records of this period is found on the slopes of Mount Stephen near Field, British Columbia. In the 550-million-year-old shale are fossilized remains of early crabs, crayfish, shrimp, lobster, leeches, worms, jellyfish and trilobites.

At one time all land on earth was joined together in a single supercontinent. Probably around 200 million years ago this land mass broke apart and the continents slowly drifted to where they are today. No one knows what caused the split or what forces still propel the continents on their wandering courses, but the plate tectonic theory is generally accepted: that earth's surface is made up of crustal plates which float like rafts on the plastic undersurface. When two plates collide, one is forced beneath the other and the earth buckles, heaving into mountain ridges. Where two plates move apart, new material oozes up from the earth's interior, filling the gap and forcing the plates farther apart.

As the North American plate slowly overrode the Pacific Ocean plate, a chain of volcanic islands erupted out of the sea just off today's B.C. shoreline, spattering molten rock over what is now the province's interior. The Coast Mountains began to rise, pushed up by the pressure of accumulated magma below. This magma solidified into a gigantic subterranean granite blister, or batholith, which now underlies the whole 1600-kilometre-long mountain chain. Later, earth spasms forced up similar batholiths to form the roots of the Columbia Mountains of the southeast and the north-central Cassiar-Omineca Mountains. The tropic sea

Drift ice after spring break-up, Atlin Lake. Richard Wright, Photo/Graphics

covering much of the prairies joined at one time with the Arctic Ocean, dividing North America into two parts and isolating B.C. from the rest of Canada. The rivers from the still heaving Coast Mountains then flowed east as well as west, depositing huge deltas of sediment along Alberta's western edges where dinosaurs floundered.

No sooner were B.C.'s mountains driven up, than gravity and the forces of nature began to wear them down. Over the centuries the softer rock cover was abraded and washed away and the underlying granite exposed. Sediments were sluiced down rivers into undersea troughs, one off the western shoreline, the other along the line of today's Rockies. The western trough later thrust upwards to form Vancouver Island and the Queen Charlottes. Still later upheavals folded the sedimentary limestones of the Rockies and shoved them eastwards over the younger rocks of the emerging foothills. For millions of years Western Canada's mountains continued to rise as the North America plate inched west over the Pacific Ocean.

But the erosive power of rain was greater than the mountain-building forces. By ten million years ago B.C. had been worn comparatively flat; the Coast Mountains were reduced to low domed hills, permitting moist Pacific air to cross easily into the interior. Then volcanic activity increased. Lava streamed from several large vents and spread a thin sheet of basalt over 40 000 square kilometres of the Chilcotin and south Cariboo. Again the earth shuddered; again the western landscape heaved. Mountains rose and rivers were invigorated. By two million years ago the bones of the B.C. landscape were in place. Only the slow, steady erosion by water and the occasional volcanic belch changed the look of the province to any degree. The land was more gently rounded, its valleys shallow and its coastline smoother than it is today: the surface details, like wrinkles on a face, were missing.

Some cosmic upheaval changed the climate of Canada and the land grew cold. The luxuriant forests that covered Canada's interior into the Arctic retreated south, as did the animals. Lakes and rivers froze, mountain snows turned to ice and seas to mush. The Arctic icecap began to creep slowly south, bringing with it an abiding winter. Elsewhere in the world some primates stood up on two legs and began to make primitive tools, but Canada was at the start of a two-million-year deep-freeze, gripped and released successively by giant hands of ice that shaped and scoured and compressed the land. At least three and possibly eight ebbs and flows of the Arctic ice sheet occurred in North America; though in the western mountains, perhaps because of the stabilizing influence of the Pacific Ocean, there were probably only two, the latest retreating about 10 000 years ago.

In British Columbia this most recent ice age began in the high mountains where winter snows accumulated faster than they could melt

in summer. As temperatures dropped each year, the snow fields thickened and compressed to ice, which, under the force of its own weight, began to flow like molasses. These ice rivers, or glaciers, ground down into the mountain valleys, growing and joining to form a gigantic ice sheet that encased all of B.C. except for the highest mountain peaks. Pushing generally south and east, this sheet eventually met the edge of an even greater mass of continental ice that had moved down from the Arctic to cover central and eastern Canada. As this burden of ice moved over the land, it picked up rocks and soil which cemented into it and, like a rasp, scoured the landscape. Existing valleys were deepened and steepened; coastal river beds were gouged down below sea level to form the magnificent fjords that notch B.C.'s coast.

Gradually, the long ice-age winter waned and the land warmed. The Arctic ice sheet melted, leaving puddles of stagnant ice across the prairies. As the western glaciers retreated, they trailed long fingers of ice in valleys and in mountain hollows, but these too melted until at last the land was free — or almost free. Ice lingered in the highest mountain ranges for thousands of years; on northern slopes, remnant glaciers and ice fields still lie, though they are shrinking.

Ice left its tool marks indelibly on the land. Where covered completely by the ice sheet, mountains were rounded into domes, but the summits that reared up like islands above the frozen sea were chiselled by alpine glaciers and shattered by frost into needle peaks, their sides scooped out into bowls, or cirques, between knife-edged ridges. Like a giant earth mover, the ice also changed the landscape by depositing its debris of rocks and earth as it melted, forming hills and ridges of moraine at the glaciers' edges. A superabundance of water overflowed rivers and streams and carved other meltwater channels, gushing away the glacial debris and dropping it on outwash plains and deltas and ultimately in the sea. Where valleys were blocked by ice or debris, the water backed up to form huge shallow lakes. Glacial till was left scooped out into hollows, grooved in the direction of the ice movement, and humped up into little oval hills called drumlins. Sometimes, blockage of old river channels forced the water to run in different directions. This altered drainage is apparent in such powerful rivers as the Fraser, Peace, Kootenay, Nass, Skeena and Columbia.

The ice age also changed the shoreline of B.C., for as the ice accumulated, imprisoning much of the world's supply of water, sea levels dropped worldwide by about 100 metres. The weight of the ice pressed down the earth's crust and the Fraser delta was lowered by as much as 350 metres. When the ice melted, world water levels rose again, and the seas rushed in to cover the low-lying land. The rising sea flooded into coastal valleys which had been ground lower by the moving ice and this action gave B.C. its intricate coastline of inlets and islands. Slowly earth's crust

Opposite page: Coast Range near Chutine Lake. Daniel Conrad bounced back and much of the floodlands emerged — a rebound effect that may still be taking place.

The land that finally emerged from the ice and floods was biologically dead. The soil had been scrubbed from the mountains and carried by meltwater into the valleys and into the sea, leaving jumbled heaps of silt and boulders. British Columbia lay bare, numb and vulnerable to water erosion; fine silt, deposited in temporary lakes and channels, was exposed when the water subsided, to be buffeted by winds into giant sand dunes and blown into the valleys. But as the earth gradually warmed, vegetation struggled back, clinging stubbornly to little pockets of silty soil. First came the lichens, then mosses, ferns, grasses, shrubs and trees, advancing northwards as the ice pulled back. Following the colonizing vegetation along the ice margins came the insects, birds and animals that today inhabit the province. Man himself was in this immigrant vanguard.

In the years since the ice retreated, water, the prime weatherer of the land, has continued its assault. Steeply falling streams and powerful rivers are mighty cutting agents, slicing canyons in bedrock, wearing down valleys, scarring the mountain faces, and washing soil into the sea. Even so, the effect of water erosion over 10,000 years has been minimal.

Apart from landslides or rockfalls, most of the dramatic changes in the land have been caused by volcanic action. At the margins of the crustal plates, the earth is still restless, and B.C. can expect earthquakes and eruptions to continue. The northern extension of the San Andreas fault line lies just off the mainland coast, and several belts of volcanoes extend throughout the province. Mountains of lava, volcanic cones, ash fall, and lava flows of the postglacial age are found around Mount Edziza on the northern plateau, along the eastern edge of the Fraser Plateau, and in a line from Mount Garibaldi to the head of the Bridge River.

The most recent volcanic disturbance occurred only about 300 years ago when lava from a small cone and vent near the head of the Tseax River north of Terrace flowed downstream, blocking the river to form Lava Lake, then invading the valley of the Nass where it spread like a huge molten pancake. This eruption happened before the arrival of the white man, but Indians of the area have recorded the event in their tribal legends.

It is doubtful that a volcanic eruption of the size and power of Washington state's Mount St. Helens will happen in B.C., for the volcanoes here are largely extinct, but earthquakes are always possible. They could be small ones, just enough to trigger a rock slide or rattle a few windows, but they could also be as big as the Alaska earthquake that caused havoc there in 1964.

To visitors from the prairies, accustomed to flat vistas, all of British Columbia seems to be mountainous. In one way they are right, for three quarters of the land lies above 1000 metres and less than three percent is considered flat enough to be arable. Geologically, present-day B.C. divides into three sections — mountains along the coast, a humpy plateau in the middle, and mountains along the eastern edge. This description of the province's geological structure is simplified, but it serves to help us identify B.C.'s several different types of terrain.

The Maritime Mountains

There are two maritime mountain ranges in the province, the Coast Mountains of the mainland and the outer mountains of the Queen Charlottes and Vancouver Island. Included among the latter are the peaks of St. Elias which rise in a sheer white wall from the Gulf of Alaska along the British Columbia–Alaska boundary. They are perhaps the most magnificent of all B.C. mountains and certainly the most rugged. Relatively young, they have been little reduced by stream erosion; Mount Fairweather, the highest in B.C., rears its snowy head 4663 metres into the northern air. The St. Elias Mountains lie within a belt of heavy coastal precipitation and well under the influence of the Arctic so that they are constantly plastered with ice and snow. The peaks on their eastern flanks are much lower, carry less ice and snow, and show the effects of recent deglaciation — sparse vegetation, low tree line.

The mountains that form the western rib of the Queen Charlotte Islands are of old sedimentary and volcanic rocks, folded and faulted together. The highest is a mere 1200 metres, but they too are rugged. Powerful cirque glaciers have scalloped and fretted the peaks into the dramatic horns and saw-edged ridges that one would expect to find on far higher mountains. During the ice age, a local ice sheet covered the northern islands to only 1000 metres, and the frostbitten summits above this sheet supported their own alpine glaciers. Because of the warming influence of the sea, the ice attack was less severe on the islands than on the mainland, and some biologists believe, from the number of different plants and animal species that have evolved there, that the southern part of the islands escaped glaciation entirely. In these ice-free refuges, life followed a separate and specialized path of evolution.

Along the Charlottes' western edge, mountains plunge steeply into the sea. Despite intense wave action there are no western beaches, for eroded sediment falls quickly into deep water and is carried off by the currents. The western rim of the islands lies along the earthquake belt that circles the Pacific, and the west-facing mountains show the scars of many quake-triggered rock slides. On the north island, the Skidegate Plateau divides the mountains from the lowland plains, which are well below 300 metres and composed of sedimentary rock and basalt overlain with a thin scraping of glacial till. Here, the ground is hummocky,

threaded with boggy streams and carpeted with forest. When the glacial ice melted, sand and gravel washed into the sea, building up the northeast tip of Graham Island to form today's Argonaut Plain. The whole east side of Graham is bordered by a remarkable beach, broad and sandy and almost uninterrupted for 160 kilometres — the result of wave action on glacial deposits. In contrast, numerous rocky coves and inlets fret the east shore of Moresby, the main southern island, and its few small crescent strands are stony.

All of Vancouver Island is mountainous except for a narrow coastal plain along the eastern and northern shores and the Alberni Valley. Of folded sedimentary and volcanic rock and blocks of granite, the intricately dissected mountains were glaciated smooth to the 1300-metre level, and the peaks above were sharpened by glaciers. Vancouver Island's beaches stretch mainly along the gentle eastern shore, but the island-studded, deeply fjordic west coast boasts a few spectacular strands, huge scallops of white and black sand, pounded by waves which travel unimpeded all the way from Japan.

Between the island and Coast Mountains is a deep depression, most of it lying beneath the sea in Hecate and Georgia straits. Ice flowing west from the mainland and east from Vancouver Island met in the Strait of Georgia to form a huge frozen river which pushed south before escaping to the open sea through the Juan de Fuca Strait. The grinding action of this glacier deepened the trough, stripped adjacent surface rocks of sediment, and humped up the baggage of its train into little islands like Hernando, Savary and Harwood. The lowlands around the eastern edge of Vancouver Island and on the mainland coast, including the great plain of the Fraser River, are all part of this trough.

The Fraser Valley itself, a triangle 150 kilometres long from Point Grey to Hope, was built of 500-metre-thick sediments deposited by the river over millions of years. Each time the ice sheet advanced, it covered the plain with a cold heavy blanket which pressed down the land below sea level. The sea flooded these lowlands when the ice melted, but the land began slowly to bound up again and the water was pushed back. The Fraser River is still building its delta westward at the rate of about 7 metres a year from soil and rocks scoured from its 1400-kilometre passage through the heart of the province.

The Coast Mountains, the great spine of British Columbia, stretch from the Fraser River to the Yukon border. North of the Nass River these fog-shrouded, deeply forested mountains are mostly ice covered and though they reach heights of only 3200 metres, they seem higher because they start their skyward reach from near sea level. Ice smoothed the peaks below 2000 metres, but those above are deeply marked by intense alpine glaciation. Between the Nass and Bella Coola rivers, no major ice fields remain; the mostly granite mountains are lower and rounded. Cirque

Unnamed peak in the Coast Range, north of Mt. Waddington. Daniel Conrad

erosion on the mountains' western sides reaches sea level in a few places, and deep fjords cut into the ranges.

From the Bella Coola River south to the Fraser, the highest summits of the Coast Mountains bow to the majesty of Mount Waddington at 4016 metres. Essentially granite, this part of the range was covered by ice to around 2500 metres and all the higher peaks bear the chisel marks of glaciation. Extensive ice fields remain on the highest massifs, notably around Silverthrone, Waddington and Homathco, though each year they shrink a little. The western ranges experience high rainfall which promotes heavy vegetation; the eastern slopes are drier, their forests less tangled with undergrowth.

Pushing up into British Columbia from Washington state is the northernmost triangle of the Cascade Mountains which extend south all the way to California. In B.C. they stretch from Cultus Lake east to the Similkameen River and as far north as Lytton. Of sedimentary and volcanic rock, strongly folded and intruded by granite, the high peaks show intense glaciation. The Cascades are strongly volcanic, with extinct, dormant and even active volcanoes in a chain down their western flanks from Washington's Mount Baker to Lassen Peak in California. Some argue that the Garibaldi area of B.C. should be considered part of the Cascades rather than the Coast Mountains because of the similarity of its volcanic history. Like Baker, Shasta, St. Helens and Hood, Garibaldi is a volcanic cone built of lava and ash. Unlike most of the others, however, Garibaldi was active during and after the last glaciation. Some of its slopes, formed on top of ice, slumped when the ice melted. Garibaldi is considered extinct, but other Cascade volcanoes, including Mount Baker which overlooks the Fraser Valley, are only dormant, and eruptions like those of Mount St. Helens are still possible.

The Interior Plateau

British Columbia's vast heartland of rolling country between the Coast Mountains and the Rockies, by far the largest of the three geological divisions, is a complex area of mountains and valleys, high plateaus, highlands and lowlands, lakes and rivers. Generally the whole region is underlain by sedimentary and volcanic rocks and covered by huge patches of flat basaltic lava. Many of the mountainous areas contain granite. Among the features of today's landscape are long oval hills — deposits of glacial debris — many small lakes, the result of ice excavation, and huge empty riverbeds, old meltwater channels. In mountains and highlands, alpine glaciation created horn-shaped peaks and fluted ridges, high tarns, hanging valleys and deep, U-shaped main valleys.

North of a line roughly from Prince Rupert to Dawson Creek, the interior plateau is mountainous: on the west, the folded sedimentary rocks of the Skeena Mountains and the granite blocks of the Hazelton Mountains; on the east, the granite peaks of Cassiar-Omineca. Dividing east from west is the Spatsizi Plateau, pimpled with many volcanic cones. Domelike Mount Edziza was formed by eruptions of ash and lava, the final outburst taking place some 10 000 years ago when the molten basalt solidified and plugged the central vent so that Edziza itself became extinct. The surrounding plateau, however, is considered to be still volcanically active, with about 30 separate cinder cones of recent age, the youngest 1300 years old. Nearby lies the brightly coloured Spectrum Range formed of yellow, red, purple and white lava flows, and on the Kawdy Plateau to the north are several flat-topped volcanoes called tuyas which melted up through the ice-age cover. The northern plateaus are covered with a deep mantle of glacial drift which has been sculptured into low hills and lake-filled depressions. The Nass River basin between the Hazelton and Skeena mountains is also volcanically alive, though not currently active.

South of the line from Prince Rupert to Dawson Creek spreads the great Nechako-Fraser Plateau. Drained largely by the Fraser and its tributaries, this is gently rolling country pockmarked with lakes of all sizes, hillocky with glacial debris, and cut by wide meltwater channels. Under the ice-age deposits lie layers of olivine basalt which form dramatic, near-vertical cliff bands along the eroded river banks. The Fraser Basin, the lowest area of the plateau, was carved by a preglacial Fraser River which flowed north through McLeod Lake as a tributary of the Peace River. Blockage of its former channel during the glacial retreat may have forced the Fraser into its present course. Near Anahim Lake in the Chilcotin are more volcanoes, domes of lava humped up 1200 metres above the plateau into the Rainbow, Ilgachuz and Itcha ranges. Farther south, light grey limestone laid down in the sea that covered the area three billion years ago forms the crenellated peaks and ridges of the Marble Range.

Perhaps the best-known part of the interior is the Thompson Plateau, for it includes the south portion of the Cariboo from Clinton to Kamloops, the Princeton-Merritt area and the popular Okanagan Valley. Like the country farther north, this plateau rolls and dips gently between 1200 and 1600 metres and is dissected by deep river valleys. The underlying rocks are more varied here, being sedimentary and volcanic, with basalt and granite in the higher areas. The ice age left a thick cover of glacial drift over the whole plateau and this was later cut by meltwater channels. The ice retreated slowly here leaving large stagnant patches and temporary lakes. Into these lakes the meltwater streams deposited their sediments and, when the ice melted and the lakes drained, white banks of this silt were uncovered. They are prominent features of today's landscape along the South Thompson River near Kamloops and around

Spectrum Range, near Mt. Edziza. J.A. Kraulis, Photo/Graphics

Okanagan Lake near Penticton. The many long lakes of the plateau — Kamloops, Nicola and those of the Okanagan Valley — all owe their existence to ice action deepening the valleys, sometimes below sea level.

The western edge of the interior plateau is clearly marked by the abrupt rise of the Coast Mountains, but on the east its boundary is obscured by a zone of highlands rising to 2600 metres and merging into the mountains beyond. Typically the highland peaks are round and smooth, and have only a few cirque glaciers. Although glacial ice did not much alter the appearance of the highlands, except for an overlay of glacial drift, it cut steep river valleys — the North Thompson, Adams, Shuswap and Kettle — and scooped out many deep and beautiful lakes — Murtle, Shuswap, Adams and Mabel. Volcanic activity around Clearwater Lake in Wells Gray Provincial Park formed several cinder cones, including the perfectly symmetrical Pyramid Mountain. All are geologically young, around 10 000 years old, and are hardly touched by erosion.

Eastern Mountains

The highlands of the interior plateau merge gradually east into the Cassiar-Omineca Mountains of the north and the Columbia Mountains of the south. These mountains are composed of thick layers of very old sedimentary deposits, large areas of igneous rock, and blocks of granite, and contain the richest supplies of lode metals — copper, silver, lead and zinc — yet discovered in British Columbia. They lie within the interior wet belt and receive much precipitation, as they most likely did in the past, for they are still heavily glaciated. The Cassiar-Omineca Mountains, rising to almost 3000 metres in the Stikine Range, were covered by glacial ice to two thirds their height, and the peaks above are sharply etched by cirque glaciation. The Columbia Mountains reach higher, to nearly 4000 metres, and were even more deeply buried by ice. Not only did glaciation splinter and erode the peaks but it also carved deep and steep-walled valleys which accentuate the drama of the mountain landscape.

Four distinct ranges make up the Columbia Mountains. The Cariboo Range is the most northerly and the highest: Mount Sir Wilfred Laurier climbs to almost 4000 metres. The range's imposing serrate peaks of sedimentary quartzite lie in north-south lines separated by deep valleys. South of the Cariboos, the Columbia Mountains spread into three parallel ranges named, from west to east, the Monashees, the Selkirks and the Purcells. The northern Monashees are bold, sharply glaciated peaks with saw-tooth ridges and steep rock slopes, though in the south, where the mountains are lower and were overrun with ice, their contours are less dramatic.

Separated from the Monashees by the Arrow Lakes, the higher Selkirks contain more varied rock from several geological eras, including two huge granite batholiths in the south. Some of the highest peaks are of quartzite and limestone, both highly resistant to erosion. Remnant ice fields and glaciers persist in the northern part of the range. East of Kootenay and Duncan lakes lie the Purcells. Where bedrock is sedimentary, these mountains are sharply pinnacled; where granite predominates, they are blunt but massive. Deeply incised valleys plunge into the heart of the range, accentuating the steepness of the mountains.

The Columbia Mountains are sharply defined along their eastern limits by the Rocky Mountain Trench, a distinctive feature of the eastern B.C. landscape. This straight, flat-bottomed valley, steep-sided and several kilometres wide, runs almost the full length of the province, extending northwest into Alaska and south into Montana. It is far deeper than it appears, for it is filled with 1500 metres of very ancient flood plain and stream deposits, plus 150 metres of sediment from ice-age glaciers. It is thought to be a series of connected faults which later sank into a trough and was expanded by stream action. Whatever its origin, it forms a natural and splendid foreground to the Rocky Mountains whose bold peaks of folded and tilted sedimentary rocks rise in an abrupt, continuous wall along its eastern edge.

The boundary between British Columbia and Alberta follows the spine of the Rockies from the U.S. border until it meets 120 degrees longitude, about halfway up the province. North of this line, the eastern slopes of the Rockies are included within B.C., along with their foothills and a little piece of the great plains which enters the northeast corner of the province. The Muskwa Ranges of the Rockies lie north of the Peace River and their 3200-metre relief is crossed by both the Peace and the Liard rivers. The sedimentary limestones of their eastern flanks have been eroded to intricate castle shapes only slightly changed by later glaciation, though south of the Alaska Highway the mountains have been sculptured by ice to provide alpine scenery as breathtaking as that of the southern Rockies. South of the Peace River, the Hart Ranges are low, mostly under 2500 metres, and less rugged, for they were smoothed by the covering ice.

The mountains that best exemplify the Rockies are the Border and Continental ranges which, shared by B.C. and Alberta, stretch from Fernie in the south to Mount Sir Alexander in the north. It is difficult to generalize about so huge an area, for each range has its own geological peculiarities, but all these high mountains are of sedimentary origin, the products of millions of years of submarine accumulation. The rock strata form many different mountain shapes — the sharp horn of Mount Assiniboine, the monumental castle block of Mount Robson, the steep escarpment of Mount Rundle — and all bear the imprint of deep and repeated glaciation. The type of sedimentary rock controls to some extent the forms of the mountains and the vegetation that covers them.

Where slopes are timbered, underlying rock is probably argillite, sandstone or siltstone whereas resistant limestone bedrock produces steep, bare slopes and dramatic peaks. Characteristic of all the Rockies are the huge talus slopes that fan out below mountain cliffs. These were caused by ice which oversteepened the slopes to the point of instability, and massive erosion took place. The mountains are literally falling down.

The foothills of the Rockies in northeastern B.C. were covered completely by the ice from the mountains which left little trace of its passage except for thick deposits of glacial till and deeply eroded eastern valleys. A tenth of the land area of British Columbia lies east of the foothills, geologically part of the interior plain that covers the prairie provinces. This Peace River corner is relatively low-lying and is underlain by undisturbed sedimentary rock containing rich deposits of natural gas and petroleum. A hard sandstone cap has been cut into steep cliffs by the Peace and the Liard river valleys. The continental ice sheet moved southwest over the plain and reached as far as the foothills. When it retreated east, depositing a thick blanket of boulder-filled debris, icy hands from Rocky Mountain glaciers reached after it, leaving moraine ridges and mounds. Outwash from the mountains flooded the Peace River area, discharging huge volumes of sand and silt into a Glacial Lake Peace whose former shorelines are still visible.

Soil and Weather

Bedrock composition and glaciation may explain the contours of the land, but they only begin to account for the differences in the structure and quality of the soils that cover it. Other factors such as topography, rainfall and temperature are also critical. These factors influence the kinds of vegetation that the soils support, but the vegetation itself, by contributing organic matter, helps determine soil fertility. On the whole, B.C.'s mountain soils are acid, impoverished by the nature of the bedrock, the cold, the steepness of the slopes, and by the rain which leaches away their minerals. Unlike deciduous trees, the conifers that cover the mountains shed no leaves and so add very little humus to the soil. Even on the drier interior plateau, the soils, derived mainly from basalt, are rarely rich enough for agriculture; they mostly support Douglas-fir and lodgepole pine forests. More fertile are grassland soils which form in areas having hot summers and rainfall too low to support trees. These dry though shallow soils, enriched by grass humus, support orchards, as in the Okanagan, ground crops and alfalfa in the southern ranch country, and even grain in the Peace River region. Irrigated, these soils in the south can be made to double their yield — two and even three crops of hay per year are common. Young alluvial soils that build up in deltas and valley bottoms are the richest in mineral content and, when well supplied

The Lieutenants, Purcell Mountains. Pat Morrow, Photo/Graphics

with water, are the best for farmland. In British Columbia, such soils are limited to the lower Fraser and Bella Coola valleys, the flats around Creston, and a few other places, and much of this land must be dyked and drained for maximum crop yield.

For the past 200 years, in man's experience, there has been little natural change in the land. Occasionally a river will burst its banks or a mountainside tumble; there have been rock slides and avalanches and cloudbursts, but generally the land seems at rest. In geologic time, measured in millennia, the land is constantly changing, if only because of water, the chief erosional agent, which inexorably if imperceptibly grinds down the land and washes it into the sea.

Rain falling on British Columbia runs off into one of three major river systems: the Mackenzie, which through its tributaries the Peace and the Liard drains into the Arctic Ocean; the Columbia, and the Fraser, both of which flow south and west to the Pacific. Of these, only the Fraser is wholly within the province. Its drainage basin lies mostly east of the Coast Mountains, though it cuts a formidable canyon through them on its way to the sea. In addition, the northwest corner of the province is within the Yukon River basin which diverts water into the Bering Sea, and the Coast Mountains themselves are drained by several short but powerful streams — the Stikine, Nass and Skeena — directly into the Pacific. The rain that feeds these rivers is important not only for its erosional force but also because it influences and sustains the total environment.

British Columbia's climate is influenced by three main factors: the Pacific Ocean; the mountains, and the northern latitude — the province stretches eleven degrees towards the Arctic. Along the coast, the ocean regulates temperatures year-round, keeping winters mild and summers cool. It also warms and saturates the prevailing westerly winds which sweep over it and onto the shore. Forced by the Coast Mountains up into cooler air, moisture vapour in the winds condenses and falls as rain or snow, depending on season and elevation. The outer mountains of Vancouver Island and the Queen Charlottes suffer the brunt of the wind's attack. The west coast of the island is among the wettest places on earth — the logging community of Tahsis at sea level averages 274 centimetres of rain a year, and the mountain slopes as much as 600 centimetres. It is this sustained downpour that nurtures the rampant growth of redcedar, hemlock, Douglas-fir and spruce that covers every west-facing slope. On all the mainland coast, rain falls abundantly, but the amount varies between east- and west-facing slopes and with elevation, the high mountains receiving more than 350 centimetres a year, much of it as snow, whereas the lowlands and islands of the southern Strait of Georgia in the rain shadow of Vancouver Island receive less than 100 centimetres.

Although the wind and the mountains conspire to dump buckets of rain along B.C.'s coast, they also help keep the weather temperate —

Deglaciated cirques and alpine meadow in Mt. Assiniboine Provincial Park. J.A. Kraulis, Photo/Graphics

the wind by its warmth, sucked up from the warm Pacific, the mountains by keeping at bay air pushing west from the continental interior — air which is icy in winter, hot and dry in summer. The coast thus enjoys an equable climate with only slight seasonal contrasts: cool, wet winters and not-so-cool and not-so-wet summers, though when rain-bearing winds are blocked in summer by a high pressure ridge off the coast — as they often are — the weather turns balmy.

Down from the crest of the Coast Mountains, the Pacific wind continues its roller-coaster ride east into the interior plateau, up and over the interior ranges, down into the Rocky Mountain Trench, and then over the Rockies where its force and its rains are mostly spent. In simple terms, the downs are all dry, the up-and-overs wet. The higher the elevation of the intervening hills, the more rainfall they draw from the winds. The high blockade of the Columbia Mountains accepts such a blanket of rain and snow from Pacific storms — an average of 250 centimetres a year — that their western slopes support vegetation similar to that of the Coast Mountains. Where the wind bottoms out in southern valleys, the climate is dry, with less than 40 centimetres of yearly precipitation, particularly in the deep trenches of the Thompson, Fraser and Okanagan rivers. In the very lowest, most southerly valleys, aridity reaches desert conditions, with rainfall less than 25 centimetres a year.

North, the interior feels the effects of increasing latitude, which lengthens the winters and increases their severity. The plateaus and mountains generally enjoy the modifying benefits of the Pacific airstream, but dry southeastern winds occasionally blow over the Rockies, bringing extremes of hot and cold continental weather. Sometimes, too, very cold and crystal clear air from the Arctic sweeps down to engulf the land in a subzero deep freeze.

The Rockies' western slopes are freshened by the last of the Pacific rains, but not much is left for them after the wind's long, hillocky journey. The eastern slopes, the foothills and the Peace River plain are left in the grip of prairie weather and suffer a climate more akin to the rest of Canada's — long, very cold snowy winters and short, hot dry summers.

The patterns of precipitation and temperature — which in B.C. change not only west to east and south to north but also up and down with the ripples of the sea of mountains — affect soil and vegetation. And the combination of environmental factors creates natural niches for plants and animals. These same factors have influenced to a great extent where the human population chooses to live. For people do have a choice. They are not bound by the limitations of natural environments as other animals are, but create their own environment wherever they go, sometimes at the sufferance of other life.

Rain forest, Langara Island, Queen Charlotte archipelago. Daniel Conrad

The Land Inherited

Red alder and moss, Graham Island. J.A. Kraulis, Photo/Graphics

*I*n a province that is 60 percent wooded, it seems sensible to describe the terrain in terms of dominant tree cover. Classification systems for vegetation zones are based on such variables as climate, precipitation, soils, geography and biology, and these factors determine the distribution of British Columbia's forests. Each species of tree has adapted to its ecological niche and has its own requirements for optimum growth. Some must have shade for their seedlings to thrive, some need direct sunlight. Some demand an abundance of water and a gentle climate, whereas others prosper in harsher conditions, surviving hard winter frosts and summer drought. The ponderosa's thick bark resists fire, a natural event in forest life, but the lodgepole pine releases its seeds only on the charred forest floor of a fire's aftermath.

Even within the extensive coastal wet forest zone, trees sort themselves out by the genetic tolerances they have in infancy for light or shade or proximity to ocean spray. Douglas-fir seedlings need an abundance of light and moisture to grow well. In the shade of a mature forest they stay small and spindly or their seeds fail to germinate, but a fire or a blowdown or logging opens the canopy in their favour. With sunlight streaming onto a cleared forest floor, seeds of most resident trees spring to life, along with the first quick cover of fireweed and trailing blackberry. Douglas-fir seedlings grow fast, outstripping all others in their race for the sun, and soon create a dense forest whose shade makes it impossible for their light-loving progeny to survive. Seedlings of redcedar and hemlock, however, grow moderately well in dim light, and when the 500-year life span of the Douglas-fir comes to an end and these giants die and topple, the cedars and hemlocks are well enough established to take over the forest. Because their seedlings are shade-tolerant, the cedar and hemlock trees will endure for succeeding generations, until the next fire or other forest disaster permits the fir to regain ascendancy. This natural succession has continued on the coast since the ice age, but it has now been replaced by artificial logging succession. Douglas-fir forests are found more commonly on south-facing slopes which in summer are drier and warmer and more susceptible to fire. Sitka spruce, another giant among the coastal trees, is choosy about its location for a special reason: it must grow close to the ocean — never more than 80 kilometres distant — in order to obtain the magnesium it needs from wind-driven sea spray.

A knowledge of the specific vegetation zones is helpful for fully understanding the distribution of British Columbia's trees, but we have selected several broad divisions which are more easily recognized and simpler to use when describing the other forms of life on land. They are: the wet forest of coast and interior; the dry coast forest; the alpine zone of mountains and northlands; the interior subalpine forest, which covers much of B.C. east of the Coast and Cascade mountains; the boreal or

Redcedar in Cathedral Grove, Vancouver Island. Al Harvey

northern woods; and the dry interior, including parklands, open forest, grassland and desert. Each of these land divisions provides a distinct environment for a particular set of vegetation and wildlife whose existence is more or less dependent on each other and on the topography and climate of the region.

Coastal Wet Forest

When one thinks of the coastal woods, the words "rain forest" spring to mind. Mature stands of virgin timber are dark, impressive places, hung with beards of epiphytic lichens, clubmosses and ferns. Trees stand like thick pillars up to 100 metres high, and sunlight filters palely through the sieve of far-away branches, suffusing everything beneath with a tangible quality of underwater green, hardly surprising in a place so saturated with rain. These forest cathedrals seem to suppress sound — a kind of reverence subdues the human voice to a whisper, and few birds sing except perhaps for the little winter wren in the undergrowth. Cheerier birds such as chestnut-backed chickadees, warblers, vireos and kinglets prefer sunlight, frequenting only the forest edges and the topmost boughs. The mossy ground is humped with decayed nurse logs, each one a green affirmation of the future. Tall, elegant sword fern, vanilla leaf (like triple-notched waterlily pads), oxalis, foam-flower, trillium and wild ginger, all lovers of the deepest shade, also flourish here.

Before loggers invaded the forest, large stands of Sitka spruce, hemlock and cedar thrived in wet coastal lowlands, and because these are unlikely places for forest fires to start or take hold, the woods often endured for 500 years. The rain forests were tempting to early loggers: the trees were huge and easily reached from the sea. Long before ideas of conservation or sustained yield became accepted, these magnificent primeval woods were the first to be humbled. There is very little virgin rain forest left now, even in patches, though mature stands may always have been few. Only when the natural balance is right and many years pass without calamity does a rain forest reach its prime.

Today's coastal woods, if allowed to grow undisturbed for several hundred years, would again begin to take on rain forest characteristics. But we cannot afford to wait: the forests of the coast are Canada's prime source of lumber. They have been logged and replanted and logged again and are still regenerating, though perhaps not quickly enough for our needs. Many are no longer natural environments but plantations. Stocked with hemlock, redcedar and Douglas-fir, they are younger and therefore more vigorous than the mature rain forest. Because sunlight reaches the forest floor to produce a more exuberant undergrowth, they are also biologically more varied. But to some eyes they are not as beautiful or as impressive.

Blue grouse

Cougar

The four major trees of the lower altitude coastal wet forest — redcedar, western hemlock, Douglas-fir, Sitka spruce — are big, even if they are not the giants of yesterday. Redcedar (botanically not a cedar but a cypress) grows almost as tall as the 70-metre Douglas-fir — Canada's largest tree; the hemlock reaches 50 metres and the spruce 60 metres. Douglas-fir (botanically not a fir) is most in demand by the lumber industry: it grows straight and limbless for about 30 metres and provides strong, even-grained timber well suited to all kinds of construction. A beginner in the woods can identify it by its conspicuous, tufted cones.

Western hemlock was once scorned by loggers as a weed tree because of its abundant growth and softer wood, but today, as supplies of Douglas-fir diminish, it is a valuable source of resin-free construction lumber and fine pulp for paper, rayon and other synthetics. Its drooping tip is a good identifying mark.

Pacific Coast Indians depended on the redcedar's aromatic, soft and lightweight wood for many of their culture's material things. From its giant trunk they hollowed out canoes and carved totem poles; they split its wood into planks for housing, carved it into masks and utensils, and steam-bent it into storage boxes. Today's lumbermen appreciate its natural resistance to rot and the superiority of its wood for shakes and shingles. Unlike spruce, fir and hemlock, cedars do not have needles but short, smooth scales. The tree's fragrance and the flat lacy sprays of its branches make it easy to distinguish.

Sitka spruce thrives on fog-shrouded slopes below 300 metres and near the sea; it finds an ideal existence on coastal lowlands and islands — the Queen Charlottes in particular — where patches of rain forest still exist. On shorelines lashed by constant sea spray it is the only tree — apart from the indomitable shore pine — that can grow at all. The soft strong wood of spruce is unexcelled for the manufacture of musical sounding boards and organ pipes, of racing shells and wooden airplanes.

Two other trees have a dominant place in the wet forest: the amabilis or silver fir, its needles striped with white on their lower sides, and the larger grand fir. The first is shade-loving and associates with redcedar and hemlock; the latter prefers warmth and light but will grow only below the 300-metre level.

Unlike the open-floored mature rain forest, the second-growth or immature wet forest seems to try to keep man out, as if it had learned a bitter lesson. Young trees and shrubs jostle for space and light under the canopy of taller trees, with dense thickets of tangled vine maple, salal and thorny devil's club — all rampant growers — forming barriers that are nearly impassable except when attacked with a machete. Only when the trees grow tall enough to block out the sun does this undergrowth diminish. In drier areas the forest edges explode into deciduous growth, abloom with dogwood, flowering currant and the heavy white trusses of elderberry. Slide areas and logged clearings are vigorously invaded by red alder and big-leaf maple which bring touches of autumn gold to the sombre woodlands. Maples seem to have a special affinity for mosses which bind all their branches with fat, spongy bandages of green.

Steller's jay

Flowers of the forest are small and usually white or pale pink, such as foam-flower, Oregon fairy bells, starflower, false Solomon's seal and wild lily-of-the-valley. In deepest shade grows the waxy white Indian pipe which needs no sunlight, taking its sustenance from decayed organic matter. Also without chlorophyll are the moisture-loving fungi; the mushrooms, with their varied shapes and colours, push up through the autumn litter of the forest floor or attach themselves to logs or tree trunks. Sunlight in the forest promotes not only more growth but also colour — the rich magenta of salmonberry blossoms, blue and yellow violets, pink bleedinghearts, tiger lilies, yellow mimulus and purple vetch, compensating a hiker with rainbow hues for the inconvenience of the undergrowth barricade. Boggy areas in spring are vivid with the thrusting sheaths of skunk cabbage and pretty in summer with clusters of white Labrador tea and the pink candy blossoms of swamp laurel.

Timber wolf

Many woodpeckers live in these moist woods including the large red-crested pileated woodpecker with its ringing call, the smaller hairy, and its even smaller look-alike the downy woodpecker, both of them with white breasts and red head patches. The Steller's jay is here, too, flashing its black and deep blue plumage while golden-crowned kinglets and flycatchers flit among the upper branches. Varied and Swainson's thrushes rustle dead leaves under bushes looking for grubs. Band-tailed pigeons perch high in the conifers, and tiny gossiping bushtits weave wonderful pendulous nests of plant fuzz and lichen in the alders. Blue grouse hoot in spring, but their hollow booming seldom indicates location — they could be underfoot or far away.

The forest is home to a variety of mammals, and because the west coast is isolated by mountains and islands, a number of different subspecies unique to the area have developed. Found only west of the Coast Mountain crest are black-tailed deer, and these are particularly numerous where forest clearings have encouraged the growth of the tender shrubbery that deer prefer. Two coast species of cougar, one confined to Vancouver Island, prey on the deer, following them from the sheltered lowland woods where they spend the winter to summer quarters on subalpine meadows. Wolves also hunt the deer, and both the wolf and the cougar pursue elk. The only remaining Roosevelt elk in B.C. are on Vancouver Island. The vociferous squirrel is more likely to be heard than seen in the forest gloom. Along the south mainland coast, the Douglas squirrel is called the chickaree because of its birdlike chatter. It is replaced along the north coast and on Vancouver Island by the brighter coastal subspecies of red squirrel. Flying squirrels frequent the mainland

Elk

Douglas squirrel

Chipmunk

Gray jay

forest, but prefer the open spaces of mature woodlands which provide room for their spectacular leaps.

Black bears are common here as elsewhere in B.C. By nature secretive, they are more often seen feasting on berries along forest edges or swatting at spawning salmon in river estuaries. Two large-skulled species of bear developed separately on Vancouver Island and the Queen Charlottes, probably because of their restricted range. Subspecies of several other mammals are found on the Charlottes and their variation may be attributable to the absence of ice-age glaciation. They include otter, weasel, shrew, a large, pale marten, and two subspecies of white-footed mouse. Several mammals are absent entirely from the Queen Charlottes and some north coast islands, among them the grizzly bear, cougar, wolf, beaver, fisher, flying squirrel and mountain goat.

As the coast forest climbs higher up the mountain slopes, its character changes, for the soil cover is thinner and better drained, temperatures are lower, and more moisture falls as snow. Conditions become critical at about 900 metres above sea level in the south and 300 metres in the north. Above these heights, the trees of the temperate lowland are supplanted by sturdier mountain species: alpine fir, mountain hemlock, yellowcedar. As the forest approaches the tree line and slopes steepen, it becomes increasingly open. This is huckleberry and mountain-ash country, the realm of the white rhododendron, false azalea and copper bush, a tough triad which often forms aggressive thickets.

While many birds, mammals and plants of the lower, warmer forest are found here, the bold gray or Canada jay is more likely to be seen than the crested Steller's, and varied and Swainson's thrushes are common. These open mountain forests provide the best chance of seeing the black-tailed deer as they wander uphill in search of better forage.

Interior Wet Forest

A forest strikingly similar to that of the coastal lowlands grows in eastern B.C. on the lower slopes and valleys of the Columbia Mountains. Although considerably colder, this forest is also dominated by hemlock and redcedar, with Douglas-fir in drier areas and western larch in the south. Sitka spruce, big-leaf and vine maples and red alder do not occur. Although these forests are less exuberant because of the short growing season, they are still dark and dense jungles of moss, ferns and hanging lichens. Missing from the shrubbery is salal, the tough evergreen tangler of the coast. Salmonberry is also absent as are vanilla leaf, wild lily-of-the-valley and flowering dogwood. But skunk cabbage is here, the inevitable companion of redcedar in swampy woodlands, as well as thimbleberry, huckleberry and a host of coastal flowers. A bright addition

Foliose lichen and witches' butter fungus, Graham Island. Daniel Conrad

Snowbound krummholz in the Coast Range. Gunter Marx, Photo/Graphics

is the wood lily whose trumpet flares to over seven centimetres of speckled orange. Birds are very similar to those of the coast forest — the Columbia woodlands are the only place in the interior to find chestnut-backed chickadees — though bushtits and band-tailed pigeons are coastal species only. White-tailed deer (not the black-tailed of the coast) and mule deer are common. Moose can sometimes be seen, particularly in weedy lakes and streams, and in winter caribou come down to the forest for shelter and to feast on tree lichens.

White-tailed deer

Dry Coast Forest

The shore fringes and islands of the Strait of Georgia in the deepest of the coastal rain shadow receive only 75 to 100 centimetres of rain a year, less than one third that of the wet forest of the western slope. Here winters are very mild, seldom dropping below freezing, and summers dependably dry. The redcedar and hemlock of the rain forest cannot survive such drought, but the sturdy Douglas-fir does, and with it, always within sight and sound of the sea, grow two other trees which set the dry coast forest apart. Both the arbutus and the Garry oak grow nowhere else in Canada and both are beautiful trees. Smooth, sinuous limbs clad in coppery bark which sheds to bright lime green distinguish the arbutus tree. Its evergreen leaves are large and leathery and its clusters of creamy flowers are followed by brilliant orange berries. The arbutus flaunts its good looks widely throughout the rain shadow region, particularly on the Gulf Islands. The Garry oak is dour of mien, shaggy of outline, with gnarled trunk and branches and corrugated grey bark. It prefers the stoniest and driest of soils, often digging its roots down into cracks in glacially scoured bedrock outcrops. While its craggy profile would seem to indicate tenacity and endurance, the tree is here at the northernmost limits of its range, and grows and reproduces only very slowly. Pure stands used to cover coastal areas of southwestern Vancouver Island, but sadly, the growth of suburbia around Victoria has cleared away much of them.

Snowy owl

The open forests and rock bluffs of the dry coastal belt are home to most of the shrubs and flowers of the damper forest, with some interesting additions that enhance the area's Mediterranean image. Only here can be found the deep blue flowers of camas, whose bulbs were once an important food for local Indians, large-flowered brodiaea, and pale purple satinflowers, more poignantly known as grass widows. Adding to this flowering display are soft pink sea blush and thrift, vivid magenta shootingstars, and blue-eyed mary. In early spring, the woods are carpeted with erythroniums, or Easter lilies, regal in white and gold. Broom and gorse, both transplants from Britain, have run wild on the headlands. Some of the flowers of the interior dry belt are here too: death

Arbutus and broom, Saltspring Island. J.A. Kraulis, Photo/Graphics

Valley of the Tatshenshini, St. Elias Range. Pat Morrow, Photo/Graphics

Raven

Red fox

camas, phacelia, blue-eyed grass and even cactus on especially dry and protected sites.

A few distinctive birds call this dry coast home, among them the European skylark and the California quail, both introduced species.

Alpine

While trees are sturdy and adaptable forms of life, on the high mountains they reach the limits of their endurance. The contour line between growth and no growth — the tree line — varies in elevation according to latitude, ranging from around 2000 metres in the south to 900 metres in the north. Above this line, the essentially treeless alpine zone stretches to the summits. Because this zone is determined principally by temperature, it is found on mountains throughout B.C., becoming more prominent in northerly locations.

Thin soil, exposed bedrock and severe weather make this alpine country the most hostile of B.C.'s zones, for the land is snow-covered and below freezing eight months of the year or longer and exposed to winds and biting frost even during its short growing season. Open slopes quickly desiccate in the wind, and the thinner air of the mountain heights lets through more of the sun's destructive radiation.

Steep mountain summits not perpetually covered by snow are arid, rocky places, able to sustain vegetation only in pockets of shallow soil between the rocks. Here the plants are low, with short stems and small leaves to cut down on wind resistance. At first glance this area is bleak and drab even in midsummer, but a closer look among the rocks reveals neat pincushions of pink-and-white creeping phlox and moss campion, alpine forget-me-nots of brilliant sky blue, and even tiny shrubs — the dogged Arctic willow. The rocks are not entirely barren, for they are speckled with crusty lichens, grey, black and green, the land's first pioneering plants. Primitive but well adapted to harsh conditions, lichens take sustenance from air as well as water. They grow only very slowly, but their stubborn hold gradually wears down the rocks to soil particles so that other plants can take root. Where summits are rounded, there is more soil and other kinds of vegetation can grow.

Farther downhill where conditions are kinder, low heathers form dense, springy mats. There are two common kinds, both with bell-shaped flowers, but the rose-red mountain heather resembles a shrubby tree with needle-like leaves which reduce transpiration. The white-blooming heather has tightly sheathed leaves like tiny scales for the same reason.

The most beautiful of the alpine areas are the damper meadows just above the tree line where the mountain slopes are gentler, and the soil is deeper. The magnificence of these meadows in full summer bloom cannot be overstated, for though their flowering is brief it is intense, with many different species unfolding at the same time. There is an urgency to this mass blooming: the plants have only a few weeks to grow and blossom and set seed while the ground is still moist and before the snow comes again. On most mountains there are two flowering crescendos. The first starts right after snowmelt with some flowers impatiently pushing up through the last of the snow patches. The colours of these first meadows of "spring" — spring in the high mountains comes no earlier than June or July — are restrained, mostly the yellow of nodding snow lilies and the blue-white of anemones. When these fade a second carpet of bloom unrolls: blue lupine, yellow arnica and alpine daisy, white valerian, meadow spirea and erigeron, the big pleated leaves of poisonous Indian hellebore, and the scarlet plumes of Indian paintbrush. Among the flowers, the tousled seed heads of the anemone, called tow-headed babies, nod in the wind. Where trees venture onto the meadows, they are often stunted or deformed by wind and snow, but beneath them grow tigerlilies and the lively red and yellow columbines. This ephemeral sweet flowering climax attracts equally brilliant butterflies — Steller's orangespot, cloudy parnassian, California checkerspot and Vidler's alpine — flowers on the wing.

Rufous hummingbird

Birds are few in this high country. The white-tailed ptarmigan is at home here, though it is rarely seen. Its brown and speckled plumage, which is perfect camouflage among the rocks in summer, turns to pure white in winter to mock its surroundings. Feathers around its feet splay out like snowshoes, keeping it afloat on the lightest of powder snow. The water pipit also prefers the cold crisp air of the mountains in which to nest and rear its young. It lays its eggs in a grassy scoop on the ground and sings only in flight. Other alpine enthusiasts are gray-crowned rosy finches, sometimes seen in chirruping flocks with mountain chickadees in open fir thickets just below the tree line. And though seldom seen, Brewer's sparrow is often heard, its song a beautiful tumbling torrent. On high meadows east of the Coast range, Clark's nutcracker is almost sure to make its presence known, for it is a big, aggressive bird, like a grey crow with black-and-white wings and a strident voice.

Clark's nutcracker

Of the larger mammals, grizzly bear, woodland caribou, mountain goat and a number of species of sheep are at home on these harsh and barren slopes and none is plentiful. The caribou, found mostly on the northern mountains and southern Columbia mountains, browse on fresh alpine greenery in summer and descend in early winter to the shelter of the forest, returning to higher elevations in late winter. Goats find safety on steep mountain cliffs but are quickly spotted even from a distance because of their prominent white colour. In winter they must find places to feed where the snow is not too deep, usually on wind-swept slopes that have adequate forage under the snow. Many goats of the Coast Mountains come down to sea level and overwinter on steep, timbered bluffs. Stone

Hoary marmot

sheep of the north, Dall sheep of the St. Elias Mountains, and Rocky Mountain bighorn sheep of the southern Rockies also frequent the alpine zone.

Mountain goat

Buck mule deer, their antlers still furred with velvet, sometimes spend the summers leisurely browsing in the high meadows; in spring does give birth in sheltered woods far below. Large hoary marmots, the whistlers of the slopes, call the alpine meadows and rock slides home but cheat winter by hibernating for seven to eight months in rock burrows. It is in search of these tender morsels that the normally vegetarian grizzly bear leaves the secrecy of the forest and ventures onto the open slopes where it digs marmots and smaller pocket gophers from their dens. Evidence of such activity is far more likely to be seen than the great bear itself, which is cautious, especially of people, and seldom shows itself by day. Another inhabitant of the rock slides is the tailless pika, a small squeaking creature which munches fresh greens in summer and in winter lives on lichens and piles of hay which it has cut, cured in the sun and stored in rock larders. Unlike the marmot, the pika does not hibernate.

Bighorn sheep

Interior Subalpine Forest

Below the alpine zone, the eastern side of the Coast Mountains starts its descent into rain shadow, and the forest below the eastern tree line is colder and drier than its western counterpart. Here grow Engelmann spruce and alpine fir, lodgepole and whitebark pine, all species equipped to survive severe winters. Although precipitation is much less than on the forests of the western slopes, more of it falls as snow, and summers are shorter and drier. This subalpine forest covers much of the high land of the interior and changes its character with increasing latitude. Western white pine and Douglas-fir grow in the south, scrub birch in the north, and thick forests of lodgepole pine cover monotonous miles. These pines hold their cones unopened for years. After a forest fire, the cones open in the heat and drop their seeds onto the charred earth. Lodgepole pines are thus the first trees to regenerate and they grow quickly, preventing other seedlings from taking hold. The sub-alpine forest supports many of the same plants and animals as the coast forest, but huckleberry is replaced by red-fruited alpine blueberry, red columbine by blue; false box, white rhododendron, bearberry and the black-berried elder are common shrubs in a generally lighter under-growth frequented by mule deer — instead of black-tailed — wolves, bears and lynx. Moose, rare west of the Coast Mountain divide, browse in the wetlands. Spruce grouse, three-toed woodpeckers, boreal chick-adees, evening grosbeaks and bohemian waxwings are characteristic birds.

Lynx

Paintbrush, aster, arnica, lupine and valerian, in the Selkirk Range. Pat Morrow, Photo/Graphics

Frost-sluff with aspen and poplar, near Fort St. John. Daniel Conrad

66

Moose

Boreal Forest

North of a line from Prince George to Smithers, the subalpine forest merges into the boreal or northern forest, a colder environment substantially altered by a far shorter growing season, for the land is frozen much of the year. While this forest of white and black spruce is comparatively dry, its poor drainage creates extensive stretches of bog and muskeg. It is generally a gloomy landscape, its soil acidified by conifers and impoverished by cold. Under the stunted trees, hillocks of sphagnum moss push aside a dank undergrowth of Labrador tea and bog cranberry. Uplands undisturbed by fire are thickly clothed with white spruce and subalpine fir whose dense umbrellas of needles shade the forest floor and catch much of the rain and snow. The ground is dry and dark, and only low shrubs grow here — green alder, cloudberry, ground birch, upland willow, squawberry and prickly rose. When fire burns through the forest the spruce is replaced by trembling aspen and lodgepole pine, a brighter woodland which encourages a profusion of undergrowth — saskatoon, red osier dogwood, red raspberry and honeysuckle. This rich shrubbery provides winter forage for moose.

The boreal forest is beloved in summer by birds. Nighthawks nest on its cool floor; robins, boreal chickadees and kinglets, warblers and flycatchers, jays and grouse are abundant, and each marshy lake has its flock of noisy red-winged blackbirds and its waterfowl. Bonaparte's gulls nest in the trees; the boreal owl hoots over the swamps all year long. Black and grizzly bear are resident and so are squirrel and woodchuck, porcupine, muskrat and beaver, coyote, timber wolf, lynx, marten, fisher and weasel. In winter when the forest seems almost balmy compared to the bleak alpine, caribou, wolf and willow ptarmigan come visiting.

In the far northeast corner of the province, the Peace River area breaks the pattern of dark forest, its parklands dotted with groves of aspen, birch, willow and balsam poplar. Into this region with its prairie

Coyote

Willow ptarmigan

Male mallard duck

climate come birds more commonly seen east on the prairies: the large black common grackle; rose-breasted grosbeak; black-and-white, magnolia and Connecticut warblers; and eastern phoebe. The jay most often seen here is the blue jay of the east, not the Steller's of the coast or the whisky jack of the southern mountains.

Southern Parkland

South of the boreal forest, undulating parkland of Douglas-fir and aspen covers pockets of the Fraser Plateau, particularly in the Caribou-Chilcotin regions. It is a bright and lovely land, dappled with trees, shaggy meadows and lakes, loud with nesting waterbirds in spring and brilliant in fall with stands of aspen gold. Douglas-fir would dominate this area if it could grow unhindered, but frequent lightning fires have allowed the shorter-lived trembling aspen and lodgepole pine to become established. Subsequent fires further favour aspen because when the tree is burnt to the ground it does not, like other trees, have to seed in from untouched areas but sends up from its roots suckers which grow quickly into a grove of new trees. The aspen likes marshy meadows and follows watercourses in the clefts and gulleys of the hills, etching the contours at all seasons with grey or green or gold.

On higher stretches of the plateau, deep dry gravels of glacial drift provide firmer footing for lodgepole pine, which soon grows in after fire and covers hundreds of hectares with its tight pickets. An immature forest of lodgepole pine successfully shades and crowds out most shrubs and flowers and keeps large mammals, including people, at bay. Along road edges and in forest clearings there is light enough for colourful blooms — in spring, carpets of dark blue lupine, red paintbrush and yellow dandelion. Emerging onto these meadows from the dark and doleful woods that fence in many of the roads of the interior is like coming out of a tunnel. Perhaps the meadows are more enjoyable because of this contrast and they are certainly less infested with mosquitoes, the scourge of all northern woods. But always, around the next bend in the road or the next fold of the hills, the lodgepoles are waiting to begin their march into the grassland. Only man's axe will stop them.

In spring and summer, lakeside meadows are starred with purple aster, Indian paintbrush, lupine and blue columbine, the bright magenta of sticky geranium, and the pale blue of wild flax. Forest edges are fringed by shrubbery of soopolallie and juniper. Birds enjoy this open, varied country, and species from both the northern and southern woods are found here. Nesting around the alkaline lakes are ruddy ducks, those raucous criers with the blue bills and stiff upturned tails, as well as grebes and coots, mallards, canvasbacks, shovellers, three kinds of teals, American wigeons, black terns and dainty phalaropes. In the forest, lakes of

68

sweeter water provide nesting sites for goldeneye ducks, buffleheads and loons, while red-winged and yellow-headed blackbirds screech and sing in the cattails all summer long. Stum Lake in the Chilcotin is the only place in B.C. where the white pelican — one of the province's endangered birds — nests, though sometimes migrants or solitary birds are seen on other lakes in the area. At first glance, the bird's whiteness suggests a swan, but its bulkier form and large yellow bill soon reveal the difference.

The southern parkland is home to a splendid variety of land birds, too, including the mountain bluebird, lazuli bunting, yellow-bellied sapsucker and western kingbird. Mammals common to the northern and southern woods meet here: wolf, moose, fisher and jumping mouse come in from the north, yellow-bellied marmot and badger from the south. Mule deer and bear are common.

Grizzly bear

Dry Interior Forest

At lower and drier elevations south and east of the parklands, Douglas-fir predominates, but when it grows in the dry interior it is shorter than coastal trees, its profile less symmetrical and its needles far bluer. Dry forests are open and grassy, with sparse, low-growing mats of bearberry and juniper. Chokeberry, black hawthorn, saskatoon and wild mock-orange grow along stream banks and ephemeral water courses. These open, fragrant forests occupy much of the Okanagan, Similkameen and Thompson valleys, invading the aspen parklands near Clinton and spotting east through the Kettle Valley into the southern Kootenays. At higher levels in the south, though below the interior subalpine forest zone,

Red-winged blackbird

Sandhill crane

Mourning dove

Douglas-fir is intermixed with western larch, which lights up the fall woodlands with its golden torches. On the lowest benchlands, ponderosa pine creeps in, gradually increasing in numbers as the altitude of the forest diminishes. On the southernmost valley floors in the driest of the interior rain shadow belt, pine is the principal tree in a forest thinning out into bunchgrass and semidesert, though Douglas-fir is still common.

The ponderosa or yellow pine is stately, often 25 to 30 metres tall, its branches twisted and irregular and its long-fingered needles drooping in thick bunches. With age, its thick corky bark becomes bright orange-red, an unmistakable identifier, even from a distance. This bark acts as insulation against ground fires which sweep often through these dry valleys. (Surprisingly, though, it can make a hot and smokeless campfire.) On the fringes of the grasslands, pines grow sparingly — the climate is too warm and too dry for thicker forests to survive — and the result is an aromatic savanna dotted with trees. This savanna was covered originally by tall blue-bunch wheatgrass, but today it has been grazed down to lesser grasses and, where overgrazed, to sagebrush. Where sagebrush grows it is difficult for other species to take hold, because the fallen leaves of the sage release poisonous compounds into the soil, inhibiting the growth of competitors.

In the spring these warm slopes are bright, first with the varnished bravery of sagebrush buttercups, which poke up even around the edges of the snow, then with the splashier gold of balsam-root sunflowers, which often carpet whole hillsides. Yellow bells, lungwort or bluebells, yellow buckwheat, silky lupine, geranium, scarlet gilia, brown-eyed susan and gumweed follow later in these flowering gardens.

Birds of the southern pine woods include the Lewis woodpecker, like a pink-sided crow, the rare white-headed woodpecker, three kinds of nuthatch, western tanager, lazuli bunting, yellow-breasted chat, and American redstart. Mourning doves and kestrels are everywhere, preferring posts or telephone wires for their perches. On rock outcrops rock wrens build their nests, while higher up, sometimes on the same bluff, rare white-throated swifts wheel and call.

Grassland and Desert

Out of the forest fringes, grassland covers the dry slopes where trees either cannot survive or have not reinvaded after fire. The lush bunch-grass of yesterday — luxuriant tufts 15 centimetres across and "higher than a horse's belly" — which once covered 70 percent of this land has been reduced by grazing to a scant five percent of its former coverage. The grasslands of the Nicola, Fraser, Thompson, Okanagan and Similka-meen drainage are now, except where irrigated and planted to hay, mostly dry scrubland, with cheatgrass, tumblemustard, sage, sagebrush

Dunes in the Chilcotin, Fred Chapman, Photo/Graphics

Aspen and tigerlily, near Kamloops. Bob Herger, Photo/Graphics

Ponderosa pine in the Okanagan Valley. Gunter Marx, Photo/Graphics

Red-tailed hawk

Magpie

and rabbitbrush, and even cactus encroaching in arid rocky areas. In midsummer these grasslands seem drab and burnt out, suffocating with the smells of sage and dry earth, but flowers do grow. Although seldom in great profusion they are diverse and surprisingly beautiful. First the sage buttercups, then sweet-smelling long-leaved pink or white phlox, the large starry flowers of ground-hugging bitterroot, which open only in full sunshine, delicate yellow cactus blossoms, pale purple phacelia, and mariposa lilies like fragile tulips. Summer's end is brightened by yellow tufts of rabbitbrush, and fall sees thickets of sumac in moist gulleys flame scarlet along with the three-part leaves of poison ivy. Roadsides are bright all summer long with brown-eyed susans, Canada thistle, gilia, and the strange pink felted flowers of milkweed. This plant grows only in the southernmost valleys and is host for the monarch butterfly, the only migrant insect, though rarely seen in B.C.

On higher grasslands, long-billed curlews and scurrying hordes of horned larks make their summer home. This is a good place to see the soaring red-tailed hawk and the golden eagle, the cheerful western meadowlark and the flashy black-and-white magpie, which is seen in increasing numbers throughout the dry interior where it preys on the eggs and young of other birds, particularly ground-nesting species. Over damp meadows, the black-and-buff bobolink sings from the air, though it is becoming scarcer as more efficient methods of haying reduce its nesting sites. Near water, summer evenings are loud with the cries of the nighthawk, but its relative the poorwill can be seen in only a few isolated locations. Clumps of thistle and gilia provide favourite food for Canada's smallest bird, the calliope hummingbird, no bigger than a thumb and incredibly light, its throat feathers rayed in iridescent purple.

For those accustomed to the claustrophobic forest of the coast, the parkland hills of the southern interior are open and exhilarating. The air is dry, pungent with pine and sage, and very clear. Introduced game birds, California quail, pheasant, gray or Hungarian partridge and chukar, can all be seen and heard. The range of the white-tailed deer here somewhat overlaps that of the mule deer though the two do not compete; the white-tailed frequents the lush vegetation of the valleys while the mountain-loving mule deer comes to the valleys in winter. Among the scattered rock bluffs, California bighorn sheep find a refuge. With luck, they may be seen in the mountains of the Ashnola region, the Chilcotin canyon and north of Lillooet. Their numbers, once diminishing, are now responding to co-operative grazing schemes, and land has been acquired for their benefit. Most visible is the band on the rock bluffs east of Vaseux Lake in the Okanagan, which regularly crosses the highway for water and in winter comes down to the valley in search of bunchgrass.

Coyotes love this dry country and so do badgers and pocket gophers; there are alligator lizards on rock slopes and a variety of snakes

Eroded hills in the Beatton Valley, near Fort St. John. Daniel Conrad

Alpine larch under Tumbling Glacier, Kootenay National Park. Pat Morrow, Photo/Graphics

including western blue racer, rubber boa, bull snake and rattlesnake. The warm, usually alkaline ponds have nesting blackbirds as well as blue-winged and cinnamon teals, goldeneyes, mallards, redheads and ruddies, and the rarer black tern.

In the most southerly reaches of the Okanagan and Similkameen valleys the aridity of the grasslands reaches its extreme in the Canadian extension of the Great Basin Desert which pushes up from the Columbia Plateau of Washington a tiny pocket of desert known as the Osoyoos arid biotic zone. A fragile environment, in danger of obliteration as agriculture and urbanization continue to make inroads, it extends north for only 50 kilometres from the U.S. border to Skaha Lake in the Okanagan and Keremeos in the Similkameen. With less than 20 centimetres of rainfall a year, the whole of the area below 300 metres in elevation was once almost desert, but the valleys have been widely irrigated for orchards and vineyards. The desert is quick to pounce back, though, wherever irrigation is discontinued, and stretches of sagebrush, antelope bush and cactus still prevail.

Great horned owl

Here in the sand the spadefoot toad digs in to escape the heat, and scorpions scuttle about. The increasingly rare white-tailed jackrabbit or hare, the smaller mountain cottontail, the much smaller harvest and pocket mice, and the pallid bat are some of the specialized inhabitants of the desert, along with black widow spiders, tiger salamanders and painted turtles, sage thrashers and wintering Brewer's sparrows. Each has evolved its own way of coping with drought and heat and winter cold.

Over this harsh, desiccated country, circles of turkey vultures soar on the wind, scanning the ground for carrion. They are all black with small naked heads, and the V-shape of their wings in flight makes them easy to identify even when they are high in the sky. Though blood-stained vultures cause an instinctive human revulsion, they are perhaps fitting symbols of the strength and adaptability and interdependence of life. Without dead creatures to feed on — and they never kill — vultures could not survive.

B.C.'s ecological variety, perhaps the greatest of any province, enhances the richness of the environment, for contrasts are always apparent. From rose gardens in bloom in downtown Vancouver one can look up through several forest zones to the alpine snows of the ski slopes. In a few hours' drive one can exchange the dank gloom of the rain forest for the sagebrush desert of the south Okanagan or the grassland hills of the Cariboo, the turmoil of Pacific breakers on a rocky shore for a placid lake or a field of cows or an apple orchard.

The great wonder of this planet — and this province — is the profusion and diversity of life that it sustains, both on the land and under the water.

Waterfall on Mt. Blanshard, near Vancouver. Bob Herger, Photo/Graphics

Life in
British Columbia
Waters

Tidepools near Port Renfrew. Duncan McDougall, Photo/Graphics

The sea covers more than two thirds of earth's surface and contains all the essentials for life — carbon dioxide and oxygen, the salts of sodium, magnesium, calcium and other compounds. Such nourishment, mostly stored there since the earth's beginnings and augmented by eons of continental erosion and biological decay, explains why the sea initiated and still supports such a wealth of life — far more than the land. The North Pacific has been a temperate ocean longer than others, and creatures here have had time to adapt to its conditions and diversify. From the swarms of microscopic plankton to the giant humpback whale, life off the British Columbia coast is astonishingly multifarious.

As on land, life in the sea is controlled by temperature as well as topography. The Kuroshio (Japan) current sends a great flow of warm water to the B.C. coast, and because water holds heat longer than air, the deep Pacific maintains fairly constant year-round temperatures. Closer to shore, the water is shallower and is diluted by freshwater rivers. It cools in winter sometimes to near freezing and heats in summer often to 25 degrees Celsius as it sweeps in over warm rocks or sand. Plants and animals that live in the intertidal zone must accept these extremes. They must also adapt themselves to the rhythm of the tides, which are regular in the open sea but vary along B.C.'s uneven coast from minus tides which expose large tracts of the sea floor to high tides which totally swamp the shore and encroach on the land. Only the west coasts of Vancouver Island and the Queen Charlottes face the full onslaught of the Pacific whose breakers, full of energy from an uninterrupted journey across the ocean, batter the shores and scour the beaches. The rest of the coast, which is mostly shielded by these islands, is a kinder country, more protective of its inhabitants.

Tidelands

As the crow flies, B.C.'s sea frontage is less than 1000 kilometres, but its coastline, splintered into islands and deep fjords, headlands, bays and promontories, is nearer to 25 000 kilometres. It provides many kinds of seashore, from granite islands to tidal mud flats, from beaches of sand and mud and cobbles to rocky shores pockmarked with tidepools.

Like the zones of mountains, those of the shoreline vary according to elevation, the highest — and driest — areas being the most unfavourable to sea life. High up, the beach is submerged only briefly at flood-tide and tidepools suffer extremes of temperature as well as changes in salinity from dilution of the sea water by rainfall. Although the daily surge of the sea assures moisture and food, only a few hardy inhabitants can survive. The middle zone, covered and uncovered by daily tides, provides a more stable environment, but more amenable still is the low tide

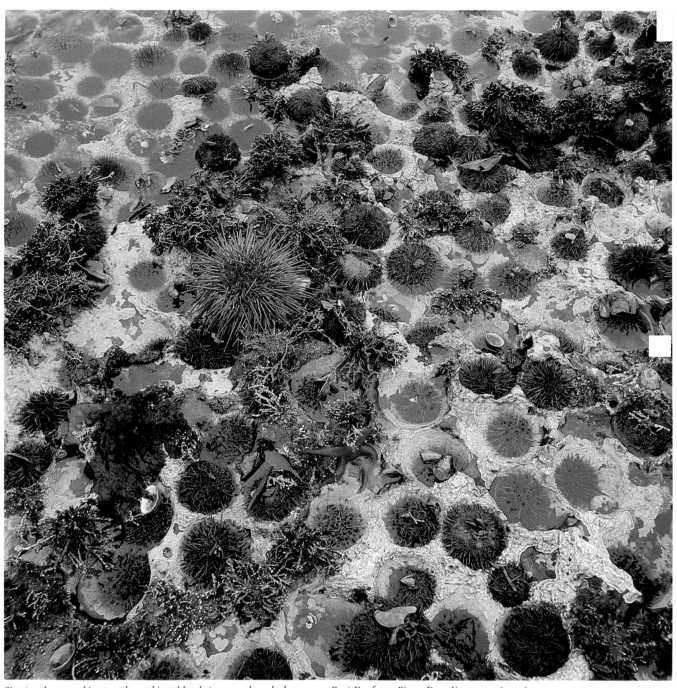

Giant red sea urchin, purple urchins, blood star, coral and algae near Port Renfrew. Pierre Dow, Vancouver Aquarium

zone, which is only exposed to the air for an hour or two each day. Here most of the creatures of the shore crowd together in much the same way and for many of the same reasons that humans in B.C. crowd into the southern valleys: the temperature is favourable and the food supply assured.

Under the sea itself yet another world exists, biologically the richest of all, teeming with life from the smallest of the primitive algae to large fish and intelligent mammals. Most sea creatures prefer the shallower, warmer waters of the continental shelf, but some live out their lives in the upper layers of the open ocean while others have adapted to the cold and the dark and the great pressure of the deepest sea waters.

Much of British Columbia's coastline is rocky, the submerged roots of granite mountains, and these shores support by far the greatest number and variety of intertidal creatures. Next to the no-man's-land between earth and sea, hardy black lichens, clumps of tenacious periwinkles and limpets eke out a precarious existence in the ocean spray zone. Lower down, the rocks are thickly clustered with barnacles, a sure indicator of the high tide zone that is inhabited by blue mussels and snails. Beneath loose rocks, purple and green shore crabs scuttle, and blennies swim in precarious tidepools. To many sea creatures, the heat and ultraviolet rays from the sun are damaging. In middle zone pools, lush gardens of sea cabbage, sea cauliflower, bladderwrack and sea lettuce provide shade for purple and yellow sea stars, anemones, mussels, goose-neck barnacles and whelks. A luxuriant mixed forest — seaweeds of an amazing variety, all colours, all shapes, all textures — grows in the low tide zone. Farther out where the waves are stronger, giant perennial kelp forms vast floating mats, providing food and shelter for a host of marine creatures and a commercial harvest for man. (Algin from kelp is used in the manufacture of products as diverse as ice-cream and paint, puddings, syrups and insecticides.) Prickly sea urchins in three colour schemes feed in the seaweed forests along with tube worms and sea squirts, sea cucumbers, spider and rock crabs, and chitons, a primitive form of snail.

In these low tide fringes of the sea there are "flowers" as well as "forests." Loveliest are the anemones, delicate blossomlike animals of tidepools and rock crevices, and masters of patience and deception. Well anchored, they unfurl their lovely "petals" of pink and red and green, and wait. When a victim alights, petallike tentacles close swiftly, stinging and paralyzing. The anemone turns into a jellied stump, swallows its prey whole, regurgitates the indigestible bits, then returns, all beauty, to its flowerlike form. Other creatures found here are the nudibranchs, some of which are like delicate floating waterlilies, though others resemble slugs.

In B.C. waters chitons are larger and more plentiful than anywhere in the world and there are five species, the biggest of which is the gumboot, fully 30 centimetres long. Armour plated, chitons cling tightly to rocks but curl up like pill bugs when dislodged. They have no eyes or tentacles and experience the world only through tiny sensitive bumps on their bodies. They feed at night, grazing algae off the rocks.

B.C.'s coast is home also to the world's greatest variety of starfish, many of them brilliantly coloured. Most have five arms or rays, but others have more. The six-rayed star is small and usually a drab grey; it broods its eggs in sacks around its mouth until they hatch. The giant sunflower star, a gorgeous bright pink or orange creature sometimes almost a metre wide, can have up to 24 arms. Like the anemone, starfish are mainly carnivorous animals and they can pry open the toughest clams and oysters.

Pools in the low tide zone of a rocky shore also hold other creatures hostage — keyhole limpets, jingle shells (rock oysters), scallops, top shells and slipper shells, tiny shrimp and even an occasional small octopus or sea perch.

The great wealth of life on a rock beach makes sand seem impoverished by comparison, as indeed it is, for few creatures can tolerate the constant shift of wave-washed sand. Only fleas live above the high tide line. Burrowed deep into the sand by day, they hop out at night to forage on piles of beached seaweed. Razor clams prefer sand beaches washed clean by the open ocean. Isopods and amphipods live at the edge of the waves, tiny scavengers that help clear the beach of decaying litter. Small shrimps keep them company.

If the beach is pure sand, purple olive snails munch on washed-up weeds, but sand dollars, sand clams and giant predatory moon snails prefer beaches where the sand is stabilized with mud. Here grow gardens of eelgrass, the only rooted plant of the sea (all others, including kelp, are rootless algae) whose blades provide homes for a vast army of crabs, snails, sea slugs, sand soles, sculpins and gunnels. Eelgrass beds are also the favoured haunt of the delicious Dungeness crab and provide food for wintering flocks of black brant geese.

Far more common in B.C. than sand beaches are those made of cobbles, rocks rubbed round by wave action. These beaches support many of the same creatures as a rocky shore, but under the stones, which shelter crabs and tiny blennies, there is a mixture of coarse sand and gravel. Several varieties of sea anemones live here and many different kinds of worms. There is also a feast of clams. The native little-neck clam lives close to the surface and so does the Japanese little-neck, an accidental import which is fast outnumbering the native variety. Both are small and delicious and known as steamer clams because that is the best way to cook them. Butter clams dig deeper in the wet mud, whereas tougher horse clams and giant geoducks live far below the surface, the only clue to their presence being a spout of water from their long siphons. Geoducks, which sometimes grow to four kilograms, are today harvested by divers who sluice them out of the mud with hydraulic jets.

Where freshwater streams flow into the sea, either in broad deltas like the Fraser's or in tiny, protected bays at the heads of inlets, fine water-borne sediments settle on the shore to form mud flats, rich with decaying vegetable matter though low in salinity. Where this mud is soft, tiny crustaceans and worms wriggle for cover under patches of green algae. In firmer mud, the ghost shrimp burrows like a prairie dog, while out in deeper water, oysters attach their rough, rippled shells to rocks or pilings. The native oyster, never abundant, is becoming rarer in B.C., possibly because it cannot endure the decreasing quality of our near-shore seas. The larger Pacific or Japanese oyster has replaced it in commercial beds, though these must be constantly replenished with seedlings or spat. Few Japanese oysters can breed in the comparatively cool waters of the North Pacific though they do so almost every year in one inlet, Pendrell Sound, where ocean conditions are just right. Oysters are grown commercially along the foreshore beaches, where they mature in four years, and on trays in deep water farms, where they are ready for harvest in two years.

The Fish of the Sea

Indians of the west coast used the resources of the intertidal shores to supplement their diet, foraging for clams, oysters and sea urchins, but their main food supply was salmon, a rich and self-renewing resource on which they depended for survival and on which their culture was based. The Pacific Ocean supports five species of salmon: chinook, coho, sockeye, pink and chum, all of which were abundant until recently. Salmon are anadromous fish, found in both salt and fresh water at different stages of their life history. They hatch in river gravels, migrate to the sea for most of their adult lives, then return to their ancestral streams to spawn and die. To the Indians, the fall arrival of the salmon swimming upriver by the thousands, each species at its appointed time, was an event that reinforced their belief in a supernatural world. Although scientists have studied salmon for many years, they do not yet fully understand what forces impel the fish many difficult miles upstream without food; nor do they know for sure what clues guide them back to the same stretch of the same river where they were born.

Chinook salmon, which often feeds in the deeper waters of the Pacific, is the largest of the species, sometimes weighing more than 35 kilograms. The surface-feeding sockeye is perhaps the most beautiful, with a blue back and flashing silver sides. Its deep red flesh is the best for canning, and therefore this species has always been much in commercial

Belted kingfisher

Male wood duck

Coho salmon

demand. While all salmon runs are cyclical, the sockeye's four-year cycle is particularly pronounced. In the climax year of the Fraser River run, the salmon, now blood red with green heads and extended jaws, swim fiercely up the Fraser and Thompson rivers to spawn by the million in a few hectares of gravel near the mouth of the Adams River east of Chase — one of life's magnificent spectacles. The sockeye spawn in most large west coast rivers.

At some time in the prehistoric past, most likely because of river derangement caused by the melting of the glaciers, the route to the sea for some of B.C.'s sockeyes became blocked, and the fish were forced to adjust to a life of total fresh water. These land-locked salmon called kokanee — a Salish word for red fish — still migrate to their original streams to spawn, but their young swim downstream to spend their lives in a lake. The kokanee is abundant in the Kootenays.

The pink, the smallest of the salmon species, is often known as the humpback because of the deformity the males develop on their backs at spawning time. Pinks do not travel far upstream to spawn, and their cycle of birth and death takes only two years compared to the sockeye's four to six years. A quick and silvery fish, the coho lives like most salmon in the upper layers of the ocean where it feeds on pelagic shrimp and small herring. It migrates up most of the coastal rivers to reach spawning grounds often many miles from the sea. Last to spawn is the chum which enters the rivers in late fall, often spawning near river outlets, though in larger river systems chum have been known to travel 32 000 kilometres.

Indians fished for salmon in spawning streams where the huge numbers of fish made them easy to net or trap. Today's commercial fishermen take them only in coastal waters when they are still firm and plump from years of ocean food.

Herring form an important part of the salmon diet and they live and feed in the open ocean, huge shoals congregating in areas where upwelling ocean currents churn up rich supplies of food. They migrate yearly to shallower waters to spawn and usually live to spawn again. Although few herring are eaten, the fishery is the second most valuable for the province. The fish are processed for oil and fishmeal and, recently, for roe. Once discarded as worthless, herring roe was found to be the most profitable of all herring products, for it finds a lucrative market as a Japanese luxury food. Herring are stripped of their roe before processing; roe naturally deposited on offshore kelp beds is also harvested.

At the bottom of B.C.'s biologically rich continental shelf feeds the giant halibut, the largest of the province's flatfish. Because these fish migrate extensively along the coast, the catch is tightly regulated by international agreement. Others of the 18 species of flatfish, including brill, cod, sole and turbot, are caught commercially in shallow banks mostly off the west coast of Vancouver Island and in Hecate Strait.

A staple of the Indian diet was oolichan, a smeltlike fish found all along the coast, and another of the freshwater spawners. It is still plentiful in the Nass and Skeena rivers where historically Indians rendered huge amounts of its oil for trade with interior tribes. The nutritious but oily oolichan is an acquired taste. Today it is caught only for local consumption.

Freshwater Sports

Rainbow trout

The rich pastures of the sea provide a diversity of marine creatures to fill man's larder, but fresh water environments are far less generous. Fast-flowing streams scour sediments from a land only recently reclaimed from the clutches of the ice age and whose cold granite and glacial gravels provide little nourishment. The clear icy water of high mountain streams may be very good to drink, but it is biologically deficient and can support few forms of life. Lakes are more productive because, like sieves, they intercept river sediments, and nutrients gradually accumulate. The still lake waters are warmed by the sun, and plankton, the base food for all other forms of aquatic life, flourishes.

There are only about 60 native species of freshwater fish in the lakes and rivers of B.C. compared to 400 in the Great Lakes of eastern Canada; most of them are smaller than a man's finger and not generally known. Dominant, and not by size alone, are trout (rainbow and cutthroat) and their relatives the char (lake trout and Dolly Varden). These are the fish most sought by anglers. Highest in esteem because of its wily, pugnacious nature and because it makes excellent eating, the rainbow thrives in the richer, nonacidic lakes of the southern interior plateau. Steelhead are a sea-going race of rainbow which, like salmon, migrate to the food stores of the Pacific and return to the rivers of their birth to spawn. Many survive the traumas of salinity change and the arduous upriver journey to spawn again, sometimes two or three times. When they enter the rivers, steelhead are big, fat and feisty; if hooked, they demand from the angler skill, tenacity and often brute strength. The Thompson, Dean, Bella Coola, Cowichan and Gold rivers are famous steelhead streams, though not because the fish are numerous. There were likely never more than a few thousand fish in these streams and their numbers have recently declined because of loss of habitat and overfishing. Rearing of steelhead in hatcheries and strict fishing regulations may rebuild the sport fishery to its previous size.

The coastal cutthroat trout also divides into two kinds: those that migrate to the sea and those that do not. Cutthroat frequent the fast-flowing streams and lakes of the Pacific slope; a subspecies, the Yellowstone, is found in the East Kootenay. The Dolly Varden char, which

Cutthroat trout

Lynn Creek, near Vancouver. Jürgen Vogt, Photo/Graphics

also has a sea-running race, is common throughout B.C. except for the Okanagan drainage. Also called the gray trout, the lake trout prefers cold deep lakes of the central and northern interior where it has been known to reach 14 kilograms on a diet of other fish.

Fast rivers and streams throughout B.C. are home to the mountain whitefish, but Arctic grayling, walleye and northern pike are found only in far northern waters. The lower reaches of larger west coast rivers, where nutrient levels are high, support populations of white sturgeon, a primitive sharklike fish which grows slowly to monster proportions — the largest recorded weighed 818 kilograms — and lives for a very long time. Fished heavily by the first settlers — a catch of 516 000 kilograms was landed in 1897 — the fishery was considered commercially extinct as early as 1901. Sturgeon are making a slow comeback and today are fished mainly for sport.

Green heron

Shorebirds and Mammals

Shorebirds, though vastly outnumbered by fish and the many other forms of hidden aquatic life, dominate the littoral scene, at least from the human perspective. Some are only brief visitors, passing through on their way between summer breeding grounds in the north and winter havens in the south. Others spend the winter along the coast, but nest around inland streams and lakes, while a few others are year-round residents of the Pacific fringe. Gulls are the most obvious of the shorebirds. The largest and most common of the half dozen species are the glaucous-winged gulls which live on the coast all year, seldom venturing inland except to raid city garbage dumps. All gulls are raucous, greedy, quarrelling scavengers, but they are as much a part of the shore as the rocks and the trees. How dismal it would be without their silver wings and shrill, sad cries. Another loudmouthed beachcomber, the northwestern crow, forages for dead crabs, fish and shellfish, though it will also snap up small live creatures and is a relentless predator of seabird colonies where it steals and eats both eggs and young birds.

Glaucous-winged gull

On rocky beaches, black oystercatchers, almost as big as crows, with long pink legs, pry chitons and periwinkles off the rocks and smash oysters open with their thick red bills. Smaller black turnstones are well camouflaged among the barnacles; larger grey surfbirds hop among the wave-dashed rocks and often ride on the surf itself. On sandy shores, western sandpipers and smaller sanderlings chase after the breaking waves. Great flocks of dunlin are also tideline feeders; they dine in unison, probing the wet sand with their long bills, then retreat en masse to digest their food, standing motionless like stones. Visiting waders of the mud flats include yellowlegs and long-billed dowitchers. Shrill-voiced killdeer plovers nest among driftwood and stones along most

Canada goose

Sea-lions off Langara Island, Queen Charlotte archipelago. Daniel Conrad

shorelines, both fresh and salt. Two ebony bands on a milk-white breast and a clear "kill-dee" cry instantly identify these birds which are common throughout the province.

Great blue herons can often be seen fishing in shallow protected bays and marshes. They stand patiently, hunched and still, then quickly stab with their long bills for fish or frogs. These elegant birds build large ramshackle nests in colonies called heronries in the tops of the tallest trees. In winter, many species of ducks, including the fish-eating mergansers, scoters, grebes, loons and the American coot leave the cold of the interior lakes for balmier residences on Pacific shores. And thousands of geese stop off to rest during spring and fall migrations, particularly on the rich estuary of the Fraser delta.

Perhaps the seabirds most intrinsically associated with the B.C. coast are those which nest in colonies on remote islands and sea cliffs, though some choose islands that are more easily reached. Mitlenatch Island off Campbell River, a provincial nature reserve, is home to colonies of gulls, pelagic cormorants, pigeon guillemots and oystercatchers; Mandarte Island near Sidney is the farthest south one can hope to see tufted puffins with their bright and ludicrously large bills, while on the west coast of Vancouver Island, tiny Cleland Island has nesting puffins, gulls, guillemots, fork-tailed and Leach's storm-petrels and rhinoceros auklets. Nearby Sea-lion Rocks, named for the animals which sunbathe there, house Canada's only breeding colony of Brandt's cormorants. Auklets and storm-petrels, like puffins, nest in earth burrows, tunnelling deeply for safety against marauding crows or falcons. Storm-petrels are birds of the open ocean. They come to land only at nesting time and fly great distances offshore to feed, hovering like swallows low over the water.

Fifty kilometres off the northern tip of Vancouver Island, Triangle Island houses the biggest nesting colony yet found in B.C. On this scrap of rock, tens of thousands of birds of 13 different species nest together, including the province's only colony of common murres, which, like penguins, are black and white and stand upright.

Nesting among the seabird colonies on isolated cliffs of the Queen Charlotte Islands is Peale's peregrine falcon, which has developed a specialized diet, preying almost exclusively on ancient murrelets and Cassin's auklets. The world's fastest-flying bird, clocking speeds of over 130 kilometres per hour, the peregrine is rare, for it has been seriously affected by pesticides. There are signs that it is making a comeback, however, now that the use of damaging pesticides have been discontinued. The magnificent bald-headed eagles are also attracted to the seabird colonies. Although they feed chiefly on fish, especially on dead and dying salmon, they will also seize live birds in the water and will fight with crows for beach carrion. Despite the encroachment of man, eagles

Peregrine falcon

Common loon

Killer whales in Robson Bight, east coast of Vancouver Island. John Ford

are numerous throughout B.C., though most are seen around coastal islands and inlets.

Mammals of the land sometimes come down to the shore in search of food. Black and grizzly bears come for salmon, the raccoon and mink for shellfish and seabird eggs, but each could easily live without such tidbits. Totally dependent on the sea for food and as a habitat for life itself are the sea mammals, few of which are seen from the shore. In the pleasure-boating waters of the south, schools of black-and-white killer whales, harbour seals with whiskered doglike faces and river otters are the ones most likely to be spotted. Harbour porpoises feed in winter in the turbulent waters of Active Pass, unperturbed by passing ferries. The only solitary large whale likely to be encountered is the humpback, encrusted with barnacles, its "spout" visible as a giant mushroom of condensed water vapour. Dall porpoises sometimes play around the bows of ships out at sea while the gregarious northern sea-lion, small of head and big of bellow, breeds in June and July in densely packed rookeries off northern Vancouver Island and the Queen Charlottes.

At some time since the retreat of the glacial ice, each of British Columbia's distinctive life zones — of the land and of the sea — achieved its equilibrium. Perhaps the balance point was struck fairly soon after the ice melted or perhaps only in the last thousand years. What is certain is that the land was rich and splendid and self-sustaining, from its forests and mountains and rivers to its ocean shores. It is also certain that nothing since the ice age has had such an impact on the natural environment as man.

Great blue heron

Cameron Lake, Vancouver Island. Gunter Marx, Photo/Graphics

Settlement

Seastack and spruce snag, Murchison Island, Queen Charlotte archipelago. Daniel Conrad

*M*ankind walked late into the New World, arriving on the northwest coast from northern Asia perhaps a mere 25 000 years ago. During the ice age that gripped most of Canada and northern Europe, some of the world's water froze, and sea levels dropped by about 60 metres, enough to turn the shallow Bering Strait separating Asia from Alaska into dry land. Much of Alaska and the Yukon lay out of the reach of Arctic ice sheets and enjoyed a milder climate than they do today. On their tundra plains grazed herds of caribou, deer, camels, horses and hairy mammoths which had crossed the 80-kilometre land bridge to escape the ice of Siberia. The bridge also provided passage for wandering bands of human hunters who followed the herds on which they depended for survival. One group left artifacts, the worked bones of caribou, horse and mammoth, by the banks of the Old Crow River in the Yukon. These bones may be 80 000 years old and if this dating is verified, it will upset many theories about man's presence in North America.

Gradually, these early hunters moved southwards down the diminishing ice-free corridor between the continental and cordilleran ice sheets to populate the rest of the American continents. This was not a mass exodus but rather a trickle of small nomadic bands, their direction determined by the presence of game and the hope of warmer weather. Unfortunately, the most recent ice advance probably obliterated all traces of early man in British Columbia, if such traces ever existed. It is certain that no one could have lived here, or even travelled through, during the years of mile-high ice.

When the ice melted, and plants and animals began to recolonize the soggy edges of the land, man slowly drifted back. The first people in B.C. probably came from the plateau area of Oregon and Washington, wandering down the Columbia River and crossing the Cascade Mountains, then moving north into the Fraser Valley. The earliest recorded evidence of human occupation of B.C. dates from at least 10 000 to 11 000 years ago.

The North American aboriginals were nomads, primitive hunter-gatherers who spent most of their time searching for food. The people who settled along the B.C. coast belong to five different language groups and show significant differences in physical traits. It is assumed they arrived from the south and east by different routes. Wherever they came from, they found a land of plenty, for rarely have conditions been so favourable for primitive man. A temperate and generous sea lapped the shores, bringing a yearly multitude of salmon into the rivers. Along the beaches, clams, oysters, mussels, crabs and other edibles lay for the gathering. There were smelt and oolichan, cod and halibut, seals, sea-lions, porpoises and whales, migrating geese and ducks — all in abundance. Bear, deer, elk and mountain goat inhabited the thick forest along the coast, which also provided berries and edible greens and shelter from the winds. Especially useful were the tall cedars with their easily worked wood and rope-like bark. The new arrivals on the coast found their two major resources, salmon and cedar, in such generous supply that, unlike most other Canadian Indians, they could abandon their nomadic ways. Once settled in permanent villages, they had the leisure to develop a complex culture.

When the first white explorers came to the Pacific Coast, almost 40 percent of Canada's Indians lived in British Columbia, most of them — around 80 000 — along the shore. The Coast Salish occupied both sides of the Strait of Georgia in the dry forest zone; the Nootka (who now call themselves the West Coast People) inhabited the rugged west side of Vancouver Island and hunted for whales in their big dugout cedar canoes; the Kwakiutl, who developed a vigorous and expressionistic art, settled on both sides of Queen Charlotte Strait, while the Charlottes themselves were home to the Haida. The Tsimshian occupied the oolichan-rich rivers of the Nass and Skeena and traded with interior tribes. The Tlingit lived along the far northern coast. The Bella Coola Indians were mostly river-dwelling, for only a portion of their territory, the head of Dean Channel, reached tidewater.

In the Interior, the Athapaskans, Interior Salish and Kootenay were less well off than coast Indians, for though the Athapaskans and Interior Salish benefited from the yearly influx of spawning salmon, they enjoyed neither the mild winter climate nor a plentiful year-round food supply. They lived an essentially nomadic life, digging for roots, collecting berries, and hunting for game. The Kootenay of the southeast were really relocated Plains Indians and were not dependent on salmon at all. They remained close in culture and dress to the Plains people, returning over the mountains each year for the buffalo hunt.

The west coast Indians were a technically capable people. They built huge communal houses of split cedar planks with shed or gable roofs and elaborately carved houseposts. They made long waterproof capes and mats from shredded cedar bark and, using the long thin rootlets of cedar and spruce, wove baskets and conical hats. They fashioned stone spears and arrowheads, bone fish hooks, and nets of woven nettle fibre. And with their stone adzes and chisels they delighted in carving wooden items that were not only useful but also beautiful — bowls and ladles and steam-bent storage boxes, huge canoes and paddles, and the posts we know as totem poles. All these items were embellished with figures and symbols of the owner's lineage, legends and traditions, the animal motifs refined to a stylistic simplicity that lifts the objects from artifacts to works of art.

The seven tribes of the coast spoke different languages, but for the most part they shared the same environment, beliefs and social customs.

Having an animistic view of the universe, they acknowledged no qualitative difference between themselves and other earth creatures, and though they depended on fish and animals for food, they also believed their quarry to be imbued with spiritual powers and of common ancestry with the human race. But there was no conflict in killing an animal ancestor for food because the animal co-operated in the ritual. For example, some peoples thought that salmon lived in a distant undersea kingdom as humans but that once a year they donned salmon bodies and swam upstream into the Indian nets. The indestructible soul of the salmon people remained in their bones, which had to be collected and returned to the river so that they could be reconstituted in human form. If any of the salmon ritual was left undone, or if the fish were treated unkindly, the salmon people would not return. In the origin myth of the Tsimshian, men once lived in peace and plenty in an earthly paradise called Temlaham on the upper Skeena River. But when they became proud and refused to return the salmon bones to the river, a great flood covered Temlaham and the race of man, except for a virtuous few, was drowned.

The bear was a spiritually powerful animal to the coast Indians, and the eating of its flesh was controlled by elaborate taboos. Called "grandfather" by the Salish, the bear was always killed respectfully, after which the hunters sang death chants over its body. All the animals were believed to have magic powers and human characteristics, and one of the most potent was the serpent Sisiutl, the lightning bolt of the great Thunderbird, who possessed malignant powers which could be harnessed only by a shaman. Sisiutl was the guiding spirit of Kwakiutl warriors. In Bella Coola legend, owls were the transfiguration of men's souls and perched on a sacred tree in the garden of Alkuntam, the sky god creator of the universe. It was Alkuntam who sent to earth the 45 animal ancestors of the Bella Coola tribe, changed to human shape. Each person's heraldic emblems celebrated his animal origins.

The raven is known throughout coast cultures as a transformer and trickster. It was he who rescued the world from darkness by stealing the sun; he who put the moon and the stars in the sky and the salmon in the sea. (The importance of the bear and the raven to west coast mythology suggests a direct cultural link with the Indians' ancestral origins in Siberia where the cult of both is strong.)

It is a popular belief that primitive peoples everywhere contribute to the balance of the ecological system within which they live by the wise use of natural resources. This is generally true, but only as long as their technology remains simple and their numbers few. On the coast, the Indians' world of natural plenty was exploited as fully as their capabilities allowed. If the salmon people swam upriver to feed them, the Indians believed it was their duty to catch as many as possible, and they did so,

Long Beach, Vancouver Island. Ed Gifford, Photo/Graphics

with weirs, traps, nets and spears. As long as the salmon bones were returned to the river for reincarnation it did not matter how many they caught, even if they caught them all. Shoals of herring were literally raked in, a dozen at a sweep. In northern rivers, oolichan were taken in uncountable numbers by nets and rakes. Huge heaps of oolichan were left to rot in pits for the extraction of their oil, a valuable trade item. Seals were harpooned or clubbed to death on the rocks; otters, sea-lions and whales were hunted avidly, though the latter only by the Nootka. Because of the steep terrain and forest cover, land animals were more difficult to kill in large numbers.

The coast people took as much as possible from the land, often more than they could use. The excess was converted to material possessions through trade and the potlatch system, for wealth determined temporal power: the wealthier the man, the greater his prestige. This exploitation-to-excess gave the Indians leisure to develop their special skills and arts. When the traders came, eager for sea otter furs, the pattern of resource barter was already well established. Between them, the Indians and the white traders wiped out the otter from the B.C. coast.

Despite the Indians' belief that all souls are equal, their social structure was divisive. A baby was born into one of four classes: chief, noble, commoner or slave, and only by attaining prestige and wealth could it be elevated in society. During a potlatch, when a chief gives away many of his possessions, a family could almost be beggared in an effort to win prestige. But the potlatch was also held for less materialistic reasons — to validate a claim to a new title, to celebrate a birth or a marriage, to lament a death, to save face after a defeat in battle or at the hunt. And it provided an important social opportunity for communion with the spirit world.

By the time the first Europeans arrived on the coast in the mid-1700s, coastal native arts were vigorous and flourishing, for the Indians' rituals of religious ceremony, their wealth and leisure time encouraged artistic creativity. The fur trade increased their prosperity, and the white man's gift of iron knife blades permitted their carvers to work with far more precision and speed, causing their arts to flower as never before. Unfortunately, the traders also brought with them white man's infections — smallpox, venereal disease, influenza and measles — which had a devastating effect on a people with no natural immunity.

Although the fur traders did little to deliberately change the Indian way of life, the establishment of trading posts attracted European missionaries in search of pagan souls. The Christians demanded total transformation of Indian society and complete destruction not only of their beliefs and ceremonies but also of the arts which held their society together. Indian culture might have survived the missionaries, but it suffered greatly when the federal government in 1884 enforced a strict ban on the spirit dances and the potlatch. For three quarters of a century, the religious and social structures of the Indian society gradually weakened, a deterioration that was hastened by the reserve system, the curtailment of hunting and fishing rights, and the education of Indian children in missionary schools far from native communities. It was feared that the deterioration of Indian society was total and irreversible, but when the potlatch ban was lifted in 1958 the artistic skills and cultural pride of the Indian people began a swift and energetic resurgence, enriching west coast life. With the reassertion of Indian dignity came a militant attack on the white man's treatment, in particular the possession of Indian lands without consent or compensation. Settlement of Indian land claims, particularly in the north, will undoubtedly have a serious effect on the economic future of the province.

The European Influence

Although the Spanish were the first white men to sail north along the misty outer shores of what is now British Columbia and the first to trade with the native Indians, it was the English explorer Capt. James Cook whose arrival in 1778 had the most impact. While his ships the *Resolution* and the *Discovery* spent several weeks at Nootka for repairs, his men bartered English goods for coverlets of sea otter fur. Later, these furs were sold for a small fortune to merchants in Canton, and the Chinese demand for more sparked the beginning of a frenetic coastal fur trade. The huge profits from this commerce for the first time focussed the attention of the world upon the northwest American coast and drew traders from far away. Mostly British and Americans, they made little attempt to explore the land or to influence Indian life; profit was their sole motive. But their effect on the sea otter, the Indians, and on the history of B.C. was undeniable.

The invasion of the Pacific Coast wilderness was a late event in the history of Canada. Europeans had been trading for furs in the eastern forests for more than 150 years, and there the lure was beaver. Unlike the pelts of the sea otter, whose fur was soft and luxurious, beaver pelts had minutely barbed hairs which were essential to the manufacture of felt for hats then fashionable in Europe. Other furs — mink, otter, ermine and fox — were also increasingly in demand because traditional sources in Russia and Scandinavia were fast becoming exhausted. The furriers and hatters of Europe came to depend on North America for their supplies, and paid good prices. As the fur-bearing animals of the eastern forests also became scarce, traders were forced farther west, travelling by canoe along the extended network of rivers and lakes. In search of new trapping areas, the British sent Henry Kelsey to explore the prairies; La Vérendrye did the same for a loose alliance of Canadian traders out of Montreal, and soon the heart of wilderness Canada was scribed by the canoe routes of

Long Beach, Vancouver Island. Robert Keziere

Skagit Valley, Cascade Range. Duncan McDougall, Photo/Graphics

the voyageurs. Only the Rocky Mountains stood between them and the Pacific.

First to investigate a route through the mountains was Alexander Mackenzie of the North West Company, an association of Montreal traders. Mackenzie travelled from today's Alberta up the Peace and Parsnip rivers, across the continental divide, and down to a broad river (the Fraser) which he thought might be the Columbia. He followed this river south until Indian reports of impassable falls and rapids convinced him to abandon his canoe and trek west through the Coast Mountains to the sea. Reaching it, he scrawled his famous message to the world in vermilion and melted fat on a rock along the shore of Dean Channel: *A. Mackenzie, from Canada by land, 22nd of July, 1793.* Although Mackenzie had found a virgin land teeming with furs, the North West Company was slow to capitalize on his discoveries, and the land west of the Rockies was left more or less in peace for twelve years. Then another energetic Nor-Wester, Simon Fraser, followed Mackenzie's route across the Rockies to the Fraser and set about organizing trade with the Indians in the country he called New Caledonia. As he went, he staked his company's claim to the new land by building trading posts — McLeod's Lake (later Fort McLeod), Fort Nakazleh (later Fort St. James), and afterwards Fort Fraser and Fort George. It was from Fort George, the most southerly of the chain, that he launched his trip down the Fraser River to find a brigade route to the Pacific. Like Mackenzie, he thought the river was the Columbia. The story of his intrepid journey down the wild river through an endless series of cataracts and thundering gorges has been told often and rightly so, for it is one of Canada's great epics. The party abandoned canoes, negotiated the terrible Fraser canyon on foot, and rode in Indian dugouts to the sea. Simon Fraser soon came to terms with two great disappointments: the river was too treacherous a route for other fur traders to follow and, since it emptied into the sea too far north, it was not the Columbia. Perhaps the sum of these disappointments sapped his courage, for though the rigours of the river had failed to daunt him, he was intimidated by the Musqueam Indians along the north shore of the delta, near today's University of B.C., and turned back.

In 1807 another Nor-Wester, David Thompson, was sent to work in the Rocky Mountain trench in southeastern B.C. He crossed the mountains with two directives from the company: to establish fur trade and to find a route to the western ocean. A Pacific connection was critical to the success of the trade in New Caledonia, for transportation from the posts west of the Rockies overland to Montreal was expensive and difficult. Thompson achieved both goals. He built Kootenay House, near today's Windermere, and other posts in Idaho, and in between fur trading expeditions he found the Columbia, following it to the sea. But by the time he arrived at its mouth, American traders were already established there at Fort Astoria. Fortunately for the Canadians, a series of calamities at the post, including shipwrecks and an Indian massacre, taxed the United States company morally and financially. In 1813, after the U.S. had declared war on Britain, they were glad to sell out to their Canadian rivals.

The North West Company then had the whole area west of the Rockies to themselves. They found a dependable overland supply route which went up the Columbia to the Okanagan, then north to a new Fort Kamloops, up the North Thompson to Little Fort, and west across the plateau to the Fraser just above Soda Creek. It was a good route, practical and economical, a combination of canoe route and pack horse trail, with plenty of bunchgrass grazing land along the way. This was the first regularly travelled trail through southern B.C. and was the nucleus of transportation patterns to come. For seven years the Canadians enjoyed a trade monopoly, but their headquarters and the political clout of the company lay back east. When a merger with their old competitors, the Hudson's Bay Company, was effected, the new combined company continued its profitable business west of the Rockies, a land that was, thanks to the HBC exclusive royal trading charter of 1821, one huge private hunting preserve. New posts were established, including Fort Langley on the lower Fraser and Fort Simpson on the Nass.

There was just one matter of concern. The 1818 boundary settlement between the U.S. and Britain had left the land west of the Rockies in dispute. Both countries claimed the area north of the Columbia River, and missionaries and other settlers began moving in from the eastern U.S. This western migration eventually turned the tide in favour of the Americans, though some historians believe that Britain's prior claim by exploration and trade was more valid. In 1845 Britain was forced to accept latitude 49° as the boundary. This left the HBC's western depot at Fort Vancouver on the Columbia, most of the southern posts, and much of the brigade trail to New Caledonia in U.S. territory. Company headquarters were swiftly moved to Fort Victoria, recently built in British territory on the southern tip of Vancouver Island, and the Columbia posts were relinquished. A new all-British route for the fur brigades was found and, though it was not as quick or convenient as the old one, it served its purpose well for the next decade. This route went up the Fraser to a new Fort Hope, then over the Cascades, down the Tulameen River, and across the grasslands of the Nicola Valley to Fort Kamloops. To supply the inland posts with meat and fresh produce, land at Fort Langley was cleared for farming.

With the boundary drawn, Britain saw the need for settlers to ensure her continuing dominion. In 1849 she gave the HBC proprietary rights to the embryo colony on Vancouver Island on the understanding that the company would bring out and settle immigrants there. Richard Blanshard was sent out from England to act as governor, but Vancouver

Island was the HBC's bailiwick, ruled by Chief Factor James Douglas, a stern and strong-willed man. Blanshard, polite but ineffectual, with few duties to perform and receiving no support from the trading company, soon returned to England, and Douglas took on the governorship in addition to his company duties. A lesser man would not have been able to divide his loyalties so conscientiously between crown and commerce, but Douglas succeeded even though fur trade and settlement were not necessarily complementary.

Colonists soon arrived to claim and cultivate clearings in the forest around Fort Victoria and along the nearby coast. A townsite was surveyed outside the palisades, and sawmills produced lumber for houses, schools, churches and shops. The colony soon had an elected assembly which issued liquor licences, sold timber rights, built roads and bridges, and generally provided a framework for civilization. From the start, the economy of Vancouver Island was based on its rich resources. Coal was mined at Nanaimo and Fort Rupert, the surrounding forests were cut for lumber, the seas were fished for salmon — and as much was exported as used locally, a pattern that persisted.

The Hudson's Bay Company has often been accused of using the new colony to further its own interests, and certainly no outside traders were permitted, either along the coast where the company maintained regular trading patrols, or up the Fraser. But it was mainly through the efforts of Douglas and the company that Britain's claim to the country north of the 49th parallel was kept inviolate. The HBC confined settlement to Vancouver Island, and without outside intervention the fur trade on the mainland continued much as before. Pack trains of furs arrived on schedule from the New Caledonia hinterland, but at Fort Langley there began a gradual shift of emphasis from fur trading to agriculture, and to the putting up of salted barrels of salmon for export.

For coast Indians, colonization brought upheaval. Fort Victoria was a magnet, and though HBC trading vessels regularly visited the coastal villages, the Indians far preferred to bring their furs directly to the white man's market where they could see and acquire many strange and wonderful items. Those close to the fort left their villages and set up permanent camps within view of the new Victorians, and every spring they were joined by Indians from the north who arrived to trade, setting up huge encampments and unnerving the settlers. Although the colonists were apprehensive of the native presence, life in the new colony was quiet, even complacent. It might have stayed that way for a decade or two, but when gold was discovered, the life and fortune of the colony changed dramatically.

The Gold Rush

For some years the HBC interior traders had collected gold dust from local Indians, but they had never suspected the richness or extent of the deposits. As the 1849 California gold rush began to peter out, American miners pushed north looking for new sources. They found gold on the Columbia and when this was exhausted they crossed into British territory, following the old brigade route up the Okanagan and Thompson rivers, then onto the Fraser where they found what they were seeking in the river gravels. Early in 1858, news of the Fraser River finds leaked back to San Francisco, and Americans, who had seen the original forty-niners become instantly wealthy, rushed to reach the new bonanza. They scrambled north by every available boat, hacked trails through the forest, and elbowed their way onto the river.

On 28 April of that year, the side-wheeler *Commodore* from San Francisco arrived at Victoria loaded with 450 men desperate to reach the gold fields. This invasion, for so it must have seemed to the 300 townspeople on that quiet Sunday morning, transformed the backwater outpost into a hustling centre. Most of the men left at once to make the hazardous journey across the Strait of Georgia and up the Fraser, but some had come to stay, for they knew that profits were to be had of a surer and more enduring nature than those in the gold pan. They bought up town lots at inflated prices from the HBC and built stores, hotels and saloons. Within six weeks of the *Commodore*'s arrival, more than 200 buildings were up, with others under construction. But these were not enough to house the hordes of miners who arrived almost daily. The overflow set up camp in a sprawling tent city. By the end of the year, there were 3000 inhabitants, and American traders had effectively broken the monopoly of the HBC, erecting stores and supply houses and grand emporiums.

The first miners on the Fraser found gold on gravel bars below the great canyon. When the lower river was all staked, later prospectors trudged upstream through the canyon to the confluence of the Thompson at today's Lytton and on to Lillooet and beyond. The higher upstream they went, the larger the particles of gold they found, which convinced them that somewhere, higher yet, lay the Mother Lode. On old maps, the names of the bars they staked and worked tell of the miners' American background — Texas, Ohio, Boston, American, New York and Yankee Doodle. There were also men of other nationalities: French, German, Hawaiian, Dutch, Chinese, as well as eastern Canadian. British miners were in the minority.

Douglas was prompt to proclaim ownership by the crown of all lands in the Fraser-Thompson region. When the newcomers arrived they

Preceding page: Grasslands near the Chilcotin River. Richard Wright, Photo/Graphics

Subalpine fir in the Sloko Range, south of Atlin. Daniel Conrad

Cascade Range near Hope. Bob Herger, Photo/Graphics

Lower Fraser Valley. Bob Herger, Photo/Graphics

Upper Fraser Valley. Richard Wright, Photo/Graphics

found that to work the mines they had to pay $5 for a yearly licence. As governor, Douglas had taken this step to ensure British sovereignty on the mainland. As chief HBC factor, he surely knew that this invasion of the quiet woods would destroy the fur-trade monopoly his company had for so long enjoyed.

By summer, with high water covering the bars and preventing access to the diggings, scores of disappointed miners returned to Victoria, penniless and unruly. Douglas put them to work building a much-needed overland route to the Upper Fraser, the Harrison-Lillooet road. The first to be built in the B.C. interior, this road was at best a series of trails connecting Harrison, Lillooet, Anderson and Seton lakes on which steamboats ran a shuttle service. Five hundred miners, each lodging a $25 security deposit for good behaviour, agreed to work on the road for only food and transportation and to receive their deposit back in food and supplies at the head of Harrison Lake when the road was completed. While this work was progressing, government officials in London suddenly became aware that the huge territory west of the Rockies, which they had thought worthless except for a few furs and to which they had granted a private company exclusive trading rights, was potentially very rich indeed. They immediately made plans — as Douglas had known they would — to revoke the HBC privilege and to make New Caledonia a crown colony. This addition to the empire would be called British Columbia, a name chosen by Queen Victoria.

In November Douglas retired from the Hudson's Bay Company and was appointed governor of British Columbia, as well as retaining his governorship of Vancouver Island. With undivided loyalty to the crown, he turned his attention to the guardianship of British sovereignty and the exercise of British rule over the thousands of rough miners who infiltrated ever deeper into the interior. Aided by Royal Engineers pressed into service from the Boundary Commission survey crew, he organized a police force, appointed gold commissioners, outlawed the sale of liquor to Indians, collected duties on all goods brought into the mainland, and surveyed townsites at Fort Hope and Fort Yale. All this he accomplished before his official investiture at Fort Langley on 19 November 1858. The year had been a momentous one in the history of British Columbia: the gold rush; the opening of the mainland to exploration; the founding of new townsites; the building of the first road; the beginnings of colonial rule. More than $40 million in gold (in estimated 1980 value) was taken from the land during the year.

To encourage settlement on the mainland, one of Douglas's first acts allowed British subjects and aliens alike (but not the Chinese) to pre-empt 160 acres of land provided that they lived on it, cut down the trees, and ploughed and fenced it. Many of the men who came in search of gold took up land instead and sent for their wives and families. Slowly the forested flatlands of the Fraser Valley were shaved into homesteads, and farms, ranches and gristmills appeared along the trails to the mines.

Mining exploration continued. Each spring a new freshet of miners poured onto the river, but most of the easy riches of the lower river were gone, and newcomers had to seek farther upstream. They explored all the brawling tributaries of the Fraser, including the two forks of the Quesnel, and pressed on into many-fingered Quesnel Lake and smaller Cariboo Lake beyond. On most of the creeks they found gold, not the fine flour gold of the lower Fraser bars, but large flakes and nuggets. The first in a series of stupendously rich strikes was made on Keithley Creek just above Cariboo Lake, where miners measured their day's take not in ounces but in pounds. An instant shantytown was built on the banks of this rich creek, and the whole area became known as Cariboo, a word soon trumpeted around the world. For several years, men continued to pour into the new colony and to trudge the 900 weary kilometres up the Fraser and along the Harrison-Lillooet Trail. A few struck it rich, but most found nothing and lost even their dreams. Gold was also discovered on other rivers: the Similkameen River near Princeton, and Rock Creek, a tributary of the Kettle River farther east.

Then the Cariboo gold rush exploded with new finds so rich that the placers on the southern creeks seemed hardly worth the trouble. Miners raced north over the midwinter snows of Bald Mountain to stake claims on Antler, Cunningham and Williams creeks where nuggets were to be had, it was said, by the bucketload.

These lusty camps in the north strained the tenuous Cariboo supply line to its limits. The way to the Fraser River was long and arduous, but Cariboo was twice as far, and there was danger that if the rough trails were blocked by snow or flood, the Cariboo miners would starve. The route from Harrison to Lillooet, the beginning of the Cariboo trail, entailed slow and costly loading and unloading at each of the four lakes along the way. Freight was handled eight times between Victoria and the Cariboo, and the cost of goods in interior camps soared to ridiculous heights: flour $2 a pound, butter $5, a box of matches $1.50 — in today's dollars roughly $50, $125 and $37.50. What the new colony needed most was a dependable, all-weather road to the Cariboo mines, and James Douglas was determined to have one. Without waiting for British cabinet approval, he borrowed £50,000 and in the spring of 1862 he let contracts for a wagon road from Yale, the head of navigation on the Fraser, all the way to Soda Creek near the fur-trade post of Alexandria. The road seemed a snail's trail on the walls of the great canyon, alternately blasted into the rock and cantilevered out over the river on stone or timber cribbings. A fine suspension bridge took the road across the river near Spuzzum, and the Thompson was crossed by boat at Cook's Ferry, later Spences Bridge. At Clinton, the new road met the Harrison-Lillooet Trail and continued to

Soda Creek, where the river was peaceable enough to allow steamboat service to the mouth of the Quesnel. From the boat landing, the gold camps of Camerontown, Van Winkle, Lightning and Barkerville, the largest and bawdiest and longest-lived of them all, still lay 100 kilometres distant. This Great North Road was completed to Soda Creek by the summer of 1864. The following year it was extended to the gold camps, but by then Governor Douglas had retired, been knighted and replaced by two colonial governors, Frederick Seymour on the mainland and Arthur Kennedy on Vancouver Island.

Still, the road was there, and Douglas must take the credit for it. Carved through the wilderness, it was the first thrust of civilization into the interior. It brought miners cheaper supplies, dependable transport for shipping out the gold, and a fast mail service — ultimately 48 hours by express from New Westminster. Perhaps more important, along the road men came to build ranches and farms and sawmills. They cut down the forests and tilled the land, raising beef and vegetables for the ever-hungry Cariboo trade. And around many of the stagecoach roadhouses supply towns sprang up — Lytton, Lillooet, Clinton, 100 Mile, Quesnel. Today, modern variations of the road are still in use, part of it as the Trans-Canada Highway.

British Columbia's early development followed a pattern: first came the prospectors and miners, blazing trails into virgin country; roads followed the miners, and agriculture and settlement followed the roads. This was true in the Cariboo, in the southern interior where the Dewdney Trail to the gold fields of Rock Creek helped open the Okanagan Valley and the grasslands of Nicola, and in the East Kootenay where gold at Wildhorse near today's Cranbrook brought about the eastward extension of the Dewdney Trail, a route now followed by Highway 3.

But there were other civilizing forces besides roads. Having so recently been claimed from the wilderness, the new colonies rushed to catch up with the rest of the western world. In 1865, as part of an American scheme to link the United States with Europe by means of a telegraph route through B.C. and Russia, New Westminster, then capital of the mainland colony, became connected by wire to Seattle. Poles rose overnight as the overland telegraph line was pushed up the Fraser Valley, along the Great North Road to Quesnel, then northwest to Hazelton. By fall of 1866 telegraph poles, like faceless totems, were 40 kilometres up the Kispiox River. Here they stopped, for the successful laying of a submarine cable across the Atlantic to Europe caused the overland route to be abandoned. But the road that was cleared through the bush became the Telegraph Trail, for many years the only access into the Bulkley and Skeena valleys.

The mainland colony took over and operated the telegraph line to Quesnel and later extended it to Barkerville, ironically when the need for

Galiano Island. J.A. Kraulis, Photo/Graphics

communication with the gold camps was declining. There was still plenty of gold in the Cariboo, but the easy pickings were gone and the extraction of deeper and less concentrated deposits required money and machinery. The hordes of prospectors wandered away, and the mining companies that replaced them contributed far less to the trading economy. Merchants in Victoria and New Westminster closed shop; freighters went out of business; upcountry settlements stagnated; the new road was neglected.

Burdened with the cost of maintaining two separate governors and bureaucracies in a depressed economy, the two colonies agreed to unite, and Victoria was declared the new capital. At about the same time, the eastern Canadian colonies were talking of union, and the new colony — now British Columbia — watched negotiations with interest. The people hoped that federation with a new Canada and a truly representative government would boost the economy and keep B.C. secure against the nagging threat of American annexation, a threat which loomed larger after the U.S. purchase of Alaska in 1867.

As far as Britain was concerned, the sooner its Pacific outpost of empire became self-sufficient the better: B.C. was urged to join Canadian confederation. Negotiations began, with the colony taking a tough stance and demanding as the price of its entry that the dominion assume all of its huge debts, double the proposed per-capita grant, and build a wagon road over the Rockies. Not only were B.C.'s terms accepted but the dominion government also promised more: in place of the wagon road, it offered a railway which it would begin to build within two years and complete within ten years of confederation. British Columbia formally joined Canada on 20 July 1871, and most of its hopes for a bright economic future were centred on the promised railway — the Canadian Pacific.

For the 26 000 Indians of the province, confederation brought nothing. As chief factor of the HBC, James Douglas had early concluded a series of treaties with the Indians of southern Vancouver Island in which he bought their lands with HBC funds and settled them on reserves in locations of their choosing. As governor, he lacked the money to extend his policy of purchase to the rest of the colony, though the allocation of reserve lands tended to be generous. When Douglas retired as governor, native land policy was administered by lands commissioner Joseph Trutch, who was far less liberal. He allowed each family of five only ten acres compared to a family settlement on the prairies of 160 acres (65 hectares). Under confederation, the B.C. Indians became wards of the federal government, which urged an increase in the family allotment to 80 acres (32 hectares). The province refused, and it was this unyielding attitude as much as the lack of land treaties which fomented discontent among the tribes, a discontent which today has resulted in militant behaviour and expensive litigation.

In the early years of confederation, British Columbia was isolated from the rest of Canada not only physically but also economically. Victoria, its sole metropolitan centre, was located on B.C.'s far southwestern edge, and so the province looked outwards, relying on overseas markets to sell its raw resources — gold, fur, lumber, coal and fish. Because of these trade ties, it felt far closer to San Francisco or London than it did to Ottawa. Gold was at first the most valuable export, worth far more than all the others combined, but each year the output from the Cariboo mines diminished and there was little secondary industry to sustain the young province. The population remained static; the economy slumped. Everyone waited for the transcontinental railway which, they hoped, would change everything. And it did, though neither the railway nor the changes came as quickly as they wished.

After seven years of negotiation and several changes of federal government policy, the railway's route through the province was finally announced. It was to cross the Rockies, then follow the South Thompson and Fraser rivers to Port Moody on Burrard Inlet. Vancouver Islanders were aghast. Since Victoria was the province's capital and its largest city, they had expected the railway to cross the Cariboo to Bute Inlet, then continue to the island to link the coal mines of Nanaimo with Victoria and the Royal Naval base of Esquimalt. When their lobbying failed to change CPR plans, they determined to have at least their own island line. They prevailed on the dominion government to give $750,000 and the province to give a land grant of nearly two million acres so that Robert Dunsmuir and the island coal interests could build the Esquimalt & Nanaimo Railway. Coal was then an important export, most of it being shipped to California to stoke the engines of U.S. railways.

Construction of the B.C. portion of the Canadian Pacific Railway began in the spring of 1880 with the first blast of dynamite at Emory's Bar at the foot of the Fraser canyon. Thousands of workmen converged on the little town of Yale whose main street was a line of cheap hotels, gambling dens, and saloons with names like Stiff's Rest and the Rat Trap. Perhaps the railway workers needed courage dispensed by the pint, for work in the forbidding canyon was difficult and dangerous: building of the railway demanded blood as well as steel. From Emory's Bar to Savona's Ferry at the west end of Kamloops Lake, 31 tunnels were drilled and blasted into bedrock and 600 bridges built across the side canyons. Tunnelling through the solid granite was slow and deadly. Each blast of dynamite hurled rocks from the tunnel mouth and triggered avalanches of debris, snow and mud, and the hospital at Yale was forced to expand to accommodate all the casualties.

While work through the torturous canyon proceeded slowly, the

Cony Peak and Spillimacheen Glacier, Kootenay Mountains. Pat Morrow, Photo/Graphics

Western larch in the Kootenay Mountains. Pat Morrow, Photo/Graphics

railway was also being built from the east. It raced over the prairies, then crossed the Rockies by the Kicking Horse Pass, the Selkirks by Rogers Pass and the Monashees by Eagle Pass. When Engine No. 148 steamed out of Montreal for the inaugural transcontinental crossing, two miles of line in B.C. were still unfinished. But by the time the train puffed through the mountains to Craigellachie, between Revelstoke and Sicamous, only one rail remained unlaid. The last spike was ceremonially hammered down by CPR director Donald Smith on 7 November 1885 and the train continued, reaching a jubilant Port Moody the next day.

Citizens and speculators of Port Moody were soon in for a shock. The railway terminus was moved to deeper waters at Coal Harbour where a new port, Vancouver, was planned on the site of a small milltown called Granville — or Gastown, as it was popularly known after its loquacious saloon-keeper Gassy Jack Deighton. On 6 April 1886, the same year that the Esquimalt & Nanaimo Railway was completed on Vancouver Island, the upstart city on Coal Harbour was incorporated. Its mushroom growth — within weeks it had 2000 people and 800 businesses — was dramatically checked at the end of June by a fire which virtually levelled the city in 40 minutes. But even this event did not abate its vigour or its enthusiasm. Vancouver rebuilt, bigger, better and cockier than before. By May of the following year, when the first train arrived there garlanded with wreaths, the youngest and fastest-growing city in Canada had swelled to a population of more than 5000. The forest was gone. In its place, 20 miles of roads and boardwalks linked hundreds of substantial homes and shops. It had a water supply system — it was not about to be twice burned — a four-storey hotel, a mayor and city council, and plans for an opera house. The new CP wharf awaited the imminent arrival of the *Abyssinia*, the first passenger vessel from the Orient, and the first to bring trans-Pacific mail and shipments of tea and silk for Europe via Canada.

The Canadian Pacific Railway was the first fine thread that, far more than any document, drew the widely spaced communities of Canada into a real confederation. In many ways it helped found the nation, but it also marked the beginning of the end of the Canadian wilderness, for across the land it encouraged settlement and speeded up the use of resources for economic development.

In B.C., the construction of the railway created an interior logging industry. The builders needed wood for ties and trestles and avalanche sheds, and their camps, many of which later became permanent settlements, demanded lumber. Forests were cut and sawmills sprang up along the right-of-way and when the railway was complete, these interior mills continued to produce lumber, shipping it east by train to new homesteads and townsites on the treeless prairies. The railway construction camps also had to be fed and this need encouraged the establishment of interior cattle ranches and dairy farms. The huge Douglas Lake Ranch near Merritt owed its beginnings to a CPR beef contract.

With new land suddenly accessible by rail and available for settlement, immigrants came west by the thousands. They packed every inbound steamer and crammed every westbound train. Although B.C. did not experience the enormous farm settlement of the prairies — its mountainous terrain was hardly suitable for extensive agriculture — still, 2000 people arrived each year by train at Vancouver, the end of the line. The stagnant provincial economy began to move.

From an economic point of view, it might at that time have been better for B.C. if the CPR had plotted a more southerly route through the province, over the Crowsnest Pass and through the Kootenays. The mountains of the southeastern interior — far removed from easy connection with the new Canadian railway — were rich in minerals. Silver, lead and zinc had been found in the Slocan; gold in the Okanagan; gold, silver and copper in the West Kootenay; gold, silver and coal in the Similkameen, and mountains of coal in the Crowsnest Pass. These remote border areas were more easily reached from the United States and it was natural that most of the mines were prospected, financed and developed by Americans. Spokane, Washington, became the mining supply headquarters, and U.S. rail spurs were built to connect the mines with railways, smelters and suppliers south of the border. (In mining camps such as Sandon and Rossland, the American Fourth of July was a holiday; special trains took miners to Spokane for weekend sprees.) To provide the mines with pit props, and mining camps with construction materials, American lumbermen cut the forests of the Kootenays and also shipped loads of lumber south for U.S. rail construction.

All the great wealth of the southeastern mountains flowed south of the border. B.C. benefited little from its own resources until the American railroad, the Great Northern, crossed the border into the heart of the Crowsnest Pass coal deposits, and the CPR, to retaliate, built a new line in from Lethbridge. This line crossed the pass, struck west through the Kootenays and then continued to Grand Forks and Midway in Boundary country. In anticipation of the Canadian railway and the cheap supplies of Crowsnest coking coal it would bring, smelters were built at Grand Forks, Boundary Falls and Greenwood. The mine owners found it far less costly to concentrate the ores in Canada and ship them east on the CPR than to continue to haul them by wagon to Washington state railheads.

The Great Northern fought to get some of this boundary trade by building feeder lines across the border at Midway and Grand Forks. It extended a line up from Chopaka and hurried it west into the Similkameen to service the mines at Hedley and Princeton. This line was called the Vancouver, Victoria and Eastern, for it promised to go all the way to the coast, though it never did.

The railway rivalry in the southeast had an additional economic benefit: it focussed attention on the mineral-rich area and brought in British and eastern Canadian investment which gradually overshadowed U.S. interests. The CPR also bought out the American-owned smelter at Trail. Population in the southeast boomed, for the railways carried settlers in as well as shipping ore out. The mining camps of Fernie, Nelson, Rossland, Grand Forks and Greenwood grew so big that they incorporated as cities. The valleys of the Columbia, the Kootenay and the Kettle were cleared for farmland, and homesteaders poured into the lovely valleys of the Okanagan and Similkameen.

When it saw the progress railways had brought to the southern interior, the B.C. government became railway mad. In 1908 it completed negotiations with the Grand Trunk Pacific to expand its cross-Canada line from Edmonton to Fort George, then west to a new port at Prince Rupert. Immediately there was a stampede for timber leases to the untouched forests of the Upper Fraser, the Skeena and the Nechako valleys, and old Fort George leapt from its fur-trade doldrums into a boom town. Soon afterwards, plans for a third transcontinental railway, the Canadian Northern Pacific, were announced. This would also come west from Edmonton, but would drop down the North Thompson River to Kamloops and shadow the CPR route to New Westminster. (The Grand Trunk and Northern Pacific railways later merged to form the Canadian National.) Construction of these two railways alone gave employment to 10 000 men and created a huge demand for lumber, supplies and food. Politicians boasted that B.C. then had more railway construction than anywhere in the British Empire. And the railway boom did not stop there. The CPR was paid a handsome subsidy to continue its line west from Midway to the burgeoning Okanagan Valley and eventually to complete it over the Coquihalla Pass to Hope. Later, the government encouraged the building of the Pacific Great Eastern from North Vancouver to Prince George (formerly Fort George) to bring the benefits of rail to the communities of the Cariboo.

Wherever these new railways went, people and resource use followed. From 1881 to 1911, the great boom years of railway construction, B.C.'s population increased by 800 percent to almost 400 000. Vancouver's meteoric rise was unprecedented. Growing from a population of 300 in 1885 to more than 100 000 in 1911, it far outstripped both the capital city of Victoria and the first mainland city of New Westminster. The city's geographical position, its fine harbour, and its railway terminus undoubtedly fostered its phenomenal growth and it gradually became the provincial centre for commerce, communications and resource industry management. Victoria's dominion in all but the political sphere began to wane.

British Columbia in the first decade of the twentieth century was a land of newcomers — Americans, Germans, Dutch, French, Scandinavians, Italians, Russians, Chinese, Japanese — though Britons were by far

Scott Cove, Gilford Island. Al Harvey

in the majority and stamped their social mores firmly on the new society. Each nationality brought to the province special skills and interests and the enrichment of diverse cultural backgrounds, though all shared common traits: a willingness to work hard and an eagerness to find new stature as Canadians. Nowhere was this grand, ethnic diversity felt more strongly than in Vancouver where most of the immigrants settled. One of the largest groups were the Chinese, who had originally come up from San Francisco to work the gold fields or were brought in from China by labour contractors to build the CPR. In 1879 there were so many Chinese in the province — an estimated 12 000 — that white workers felt their jobs were threatened and pressured the government into imposing an immigrant tax that at one time reached $500 a head. Despite these restrictions, Chinese people continued to arrive in Vancouver, and the city's Chinatown — the urban offshoot of rail camp and mining town ghettos — took them in. (Today's Chinatown, a thriving cultural enclave, is the second largest in North America; only San Francisco's is larger.)

In those boom years, B.C.'s economy remained resource-based, with mining and forestry pre-eminent. Mineral output from the southeast soon topped gold shipments from the Cariboo, and silver, lead and zinc from the prodigious Sullivan mine at Kimberley outstripped them all.

In spite of the railways' stimulation of the interior woods industry, coastal forests continued to provide by far the greatest output of the province's timber, for they were still the finest stands and the easiest to reach and transport by sea. American lumbermen were quick to realize the magnificence of B.C.'s timberlands, and the provincial government leased them huge tracts of prime Douglas-fir and redcedar. Much of this lumber was exported from Pacific ports to Britain (made closer by the completion of the Panama Canal), Australia, China and South America, though during the peak years of prairie settlement, shipments east by train exceeded ocean exports.

Sawmilling was the earliest and still is the most significant forest industry, and though the largest mills remained on the lower mainland, small communities throughout B.C. became dependent upon the industry for their economic survival. Along the coast, cedar shingle mills and plywood plants were established, together with the first pulp and paper mills. These were limited to tidewater because of cheap transportation and the ready availability of logs and fresh mountain water. Not until the middle of the century, when the industry began to use the waste wood from sawmills and converted to a less water-consumptive process, was it feasible to locate pulp and paper mills in the interior.

The first commercial salmon cannery was established in the Fraser mouth in 1867, and salmon canning soon became increasingly important to the B.C. export economy. Most of the first factories were built with U.S. investment money because California was the prime market. But when the export emphasis shifted and Britain became the

West Coast of Vancouver Island. J.A. Kraulis, Photo/Graphics

chief salmon consumer, British interests took control of the industry and many of the canneries consolidated into one large Vancouver-based company. At the time, it was believed the salmon resource was inexhaustible and during the fishing season, the canneries worked around the clock.

Agriculture was a stabilizing force in the growing province, and all good farmland in the Fraser Valley and the southern interior was soon claimed. The natural grasslands of the interior plateau became home to some of the world's largest cattle ranches; the Fraser Valley attracted dairy farmers; the south Okanagan was subdivided and irrigated for orchards, and grain was grown on 10 000 hectares of reclaimed floodland near Creston. (The development of the Peace River agricultural lands was yet to come.)

By 1910 the basic economy of the province, its transportation routes, and areas of settlement were pretty well determined. Vancouver and the Lower Mainland were physically and economically dominant. People clustered in the mild southern valleys, and the railways linked their resource industries to the rest of Canada. The later emergence of a road network and truck transportation system merely extended this pattern, for villages built along the rail routes had become too big to be by-passed, and many of the roads by necessity followed the rail lines through the mountain passes. Steamships and ferries linked the major Vancouver Island cities of Victoria and Nanaimo to the Lower Mainland and provided service to offshore islands and coastal settlements. Eventually, airplanes would reach even the remotest areas and play a vital role in opening up the north.

Today Vancouver is the third largest city in Canada, home to half the province's population. Only in the last decade have other urban centres in the interior, particularly Prince George and Kamloops, begun to approach metropolitan size and self-sufficiency. The lightly populated northern third of the province with its reserves of coal, oil, natural gas and minerals and its large stands of untouched timber, has seen only the beginning of resource exploitation. Barring economic collapse, it seems likely that further development of the north will soon swing the axis of the provincial economy away from the south. But it is doubtful that population patterns will ever substantially change.

What a country of opportunity British Columbia has been for thousands of immigrants. It gave them valley farmland, forests, minerals, fish, clean air and water. There were jobs, security, even a sense of adventure in frontier communities so recently claimed from the bush. Pioneer enthusiasm and a belief that the land's resources were unlimited led to rapid economic expansion and population growth, both signs of prosperity. But the conquest of the wilderness that began 150 years ago was not accomplished without environmental loss.

Pool in the Tseax lava fields, Nass Valley. Daniel Conrad

The Legacy

West coast of Vancouver Island. Robert Keziere

*B*ritish Columbia is one of the most beautiful — and most fortunate — regions of the industrialized world: it has wilderness still unspoiled and rich resources yet to be garnered. Its fortune is due partly to the difficult nature of its terrain and partly to the fact that man was a latecomer here and consequently industrial development was recent. This tardiness has been providential: methods of conservation (mostly learned the hard way, by trial and error) and the technology required to make conservation work are advancing each year. The 1980s bring increasing public awareness of the need to balance resource use against factors other than economic gain — the survival needs of wildlife as well as man, and the preservation of as much natural environment as is possible.

Still, any inventory of resources must be tallied honestly, with assets on one side and losses and liabilities on the other. Past profligate use has squandered much of the province's great natural wealth, a situation which we are now trying to redress. We cannot be held accountable for history, but we are most certainly answerable for the present, and as custodians of the future, we face a heightening challenge as the numbers of people in the province increase — Canada's population is predicted to double by the year 2000 — and their needs for materials, energy, food and even living space proliferate. B.C.'s generous endowment of resources must be used wisely if this challenge is to be met.

The Forests

Almost 60 percent of British Columbia — a total of 52 billion hectares — is forested, so it is hardly surprising that forestry plays the dominant role in the economic expansion and well-being of the province. B.C.'s forests grow 40 percent of Canada's lumber, much of it taken from the prolific coastal woods.

When the province first recognized the great wealth of its forests, everyone believed that there was more than enough wood to meet the needs of expanding local as well as world markets. A hundred years ago, the forests had been cut only in the southern valleys and along the accessible southern coast; elsewhere they seemed illimitable, stretching for endless green distances along the shore and climbing high onto the shoulders of every mountain. In 1885 the provincial government wisely decided to keep all forested lands under public ownership and control, and to sell or lease only the rights to the timber. By then, five percent of the forest had passed into private hands, most of it in the coast zone which accounts for one sixth of the provincial forest area but which traditionally produces more than half the cut.

Although it owned most of the forests, the government exercised few controls in the early years of B.C. logging. By the turn of the century, the economy was already dependent on the woods, yet the logging companies' "cut and get out" policy gave them quick profits and left the forests brutally scarred. The common practice of clear cutting huge areas — everything cut but only the valuable timber removed — was devastating. Uncontrolled slash burning generated intense ground heat which incinerated not only the logging debris but also humus and soil accumulated over thousands of years. Without ground cover, the soil on mountain slopes washed away with the rain, leaving only bare rock and patches of soil too thin to grow big conifers. Silt and debris sluiced from the denuded slopes into streams, damaging spawning beds for generations of salmon. And no replanting was done.

Logging in B.C. at first took place mostly within reach of tidewater where transportation by raft was cheap and easy. Bull teams and horses provided haulage along primitive skid roads, and man with his hand axe lent the falling power. Railways took logging into the interior, but only when the industry became mechanized were large-scale operations possible away from the mainline transportation routes. When steam engines replaced horses, man's impact on the forest accelerated dramatically. It increased still further when truck transport, roads and chain saws took logging operations higher up the mountains and to the headwaters of valley streams. By 1942 the B.C. forestry branch was alarmed that "our visible resources have shrunk from 250 years' supply to 33 years' supply." Even then, apparently nothing was done to curb the harvest or to insist on less wasteful cutting, and only a small program of replanting had been started.

With huge sawmills and pulp and paper mills relying on an assured supply of timber, and communities dependent in turn on the mills, the B.C. government in the 1950s instituted a program of long-term forest management and sustained yield. Officials meant to balance the amount of timber cut each year with the forest's natural growth rate, but this balancing act depended on accurate assessments of the amount of merchantable timber in the forest, making allowances for loss by fire and disease. This inventory, difficult to complete, was often inaccurate, and the forests were given credit for faster growth than they could possibly attain. Despite the government's good intentions and increased tree planting, the forest resource continued to dwindle, particularly the Douglas-fir of the coast. Douglas-fir is the most valuable of all B.C.'s timber trees, but it accounts for only 7 percent of the forest by volume. It used to provide more than one third of the provincial cut; in 1980, the harvest dropped to less than 12 percent.

In 1972 the B.C. government set out to improve logging practices by limiting clear cutting to areas under 80 hectares and increasing both the standards and controls on logging and replanting. Still, the forests diminished. However, in the late 1970s the chief export market for B.C.

lumber, the U.S. home construction industry, seriously declined, and the 1980 harvest of 75 million cubic metres of timber was down 1.5 million cubic metres from the previous year.

In addition to the 187 000 hectares of forest logged in 1980, a further 65 000 hectares were destroyed by fire. In British Columbia, 40 percent of forest fires occur naturally, usually because of lightning strikes, but these natural fires — mostly in isolated areas of the interior — cause 90 percent of the damage. Provincial forest-fire prevention and control programs are doing much to lessen forest loss by fire; suppression costs in 1980 neared $27 million.

Of the forests logged in 1980, about one third — 64 000 hectares — were replanted, a continuation of the previous five-year average. Serious replanting began only in the late 1940s. Before then, logged or burned forests were for the most part left to regenerate naturally. Although immense improvements in reforestation have taken place since then (75 million trees are now planted annually), the yearly cut still exceeds replanting. Because of differences in soil, climate, disease and planting care, the replanting success rate — the percentage of the young trees that survive — is highly variable, but the average is believed to be disappointingly low. Natural regeneration is 45 to 86 percent effective, depending on region, but there seem to be no statistics to show the additional amount of time that this process needs.

The forest industry and related businesses account for 50 cents of every dollar earned in B.C. They employ some 94 000 people and in 1980 generated exports of $5.6 billion. The forests are critical to the province's economy, yet continued decline of the forest resource seems inevitable. What is needed now to forestall future timber shortages, says the provincial Ministry of Forests, is intensive forest management which must be put into effect at once. Forest management, or silviculture, entails the breeding of improved trees and cultivation and fertilizing of the new trees in plantations. These trees are cut at their timber prime rather than being left to reach full maturity (mature specimens have almost stopped growing) and are harvested like crops of grain or cabbages, though in 90-year rather than annual cycles. Forests of this kind are grown successfully in northern Europe and the United States where the demand for wood exceeds the generation capacity of natural woodlands.

A start has already been made on tree farming in B.C. Seed from superior trees is collected in large seed orchards, and seedlings are being grown in numerous nurseries throughout the province. Newly planted forests are thinned, fertilized, pruned, controlled for mistletoe and sprayed for pests and diseases. But even if silviculture is dramatically increased, it seems unlikely that B.C.'s forests can ever be established on a true sustained yield basis.

Tree farming is one solution to the problem of the diminishing

forest resource. Another could be the release and future management of the 4.5 million hectares presently protected in parks and reserves, a consideration that few people would find acceptable. Which will be more important in the long run: the economic stability of the province or the preservation of the natural mature forests and the wildlife they sustain? The decision will not be an easy one.

Mining

It was the great mineral wealth of the mountains — gold — which first pushed British Columbia along the road to development and settlement, and mining has continued to be vital to the province's economy: today, it is second only to the forest industry. The province is well endowed with a variety of minerals, many of which have more recently eclipsed gold in importance. Today, copper and coal are the leaders, with B.C. copper in 1981 valued at around $700 million and coal at $500 million. More than 80 percent of the copper is shipped to Japan, making B.C. the world's largest exporter of copper concentrates. Japan is also the chief customer for B.C. metallurgical coal. In addition, B.C. mines antimony, asbestos, cadmium, gold, gypsum, iron, lead, mercury, molybdenum, nickel, silver, tungsten and zinc.

By its very nature, mining changes the environment. Early miners were ignorant of the effects of their placers and hydraulic hoses on streambed gravels and were blind to the visual degradation and polluting effects of tailings, slag heaps and settling ponds. The damage inflicted by smelter emissions was considered unavoidable. By 1931, with the gold rush far behind, nearly half of B.C.'s mineral output came from the Sullivan mine at Kimberley which shipped its huge ore loads of silver, lead and zinc to the CPR smelter at Trail, the province's first industrial city. When the huge Cominco smokestacks on the hill were belching, the people of Trail were assured of a good livelihood. But as anyone who travels in the area can see, this assurance was bought at great cost to the environment. The plumes of steam contained strong concentrations of sulphur dioxide which gradually killed the trees on the surrounding mountains and drifted south to damage forests in Montana. Cominco, under pressure from the United States, began a costly research program to clean the smelter emissions — and earned an unexpected financial reward. The recovered sulphur along with other wastes could be processed into fertilizer, now a profitable sideline of the company.

Until the 1950s most hardrock mining took place underground, but with world demand for minerals increasing it became feasible to extract lower grade ores in open-pit and strip mines. At first, the resulting gigantic excavations surrounded by mountains of tailings were left to heal themselves but, as a sign of changing sensibilities, these eyesores

Opposite page: Larches in the Kootenay Mountains. Pat Morrow, Photo/Graphics

137

West Coast of Graham Island. Daniel Conrad

were soon considered unacceptable. The provincial government made reclamation of all mining areas mandatory, and mining companies seem willing to co-operate. Earth is moved to sculpture the land into more natural contours and planted with grass and trees. Deep pits are turned into lakes and stocked with fish. In time, native plants and wildlife will come back and the land, minus its ores, will return to full integrated use, for recreation, for wild birds and animals, for grazing cattle or for forestry.

B.C.'s generous heritage of mineral wealth will be drawn upon increasingly in the future, particularly in the north. The impact of mining on the natural environment must be rigorously monitored and regulated for minimum ecological damage.

Agriculture

In all the great length and breadth of British Columbia, less than 3 percent of the land is suitable for farming (and only half of this is currently under cultivation); another 14 percent is grazing land. The rest, constrained by steep terrain, poor soil and short growing seasons, is agriculturally useless. It is therefore surprising that farming is the third largest factor in the provincial economy. In 1980, farm output totalled nearly $750 million from a diversity of products.

Over the years, large amounts of the province's fertile farmland have been lost to urban growth, a phenomenon which is world wide and increasingly serious in view of future world food needs. B.C.'s agricultural land loss has been particularly acute in the lower Fraser Valley which contains 30 percent of the province's improved farmland, produces nearly 60 percent of its agricultural output, and houses 50 percent of its population. Farmland has also been depleted in the Okanagan Valley and on Vancouver Island.

In the late 1960s and early 1970s agricultural land was being taken out of production at the rate of more than 4000 hectares a year. In 1972 an alarming 6000 hectares was lost. Realizing B.C.'s chronic shortage of farmland, the government passed the Land Commission Act in 1973 to prevent further encroachment by suburbia. This "farm freeze," still in effect, is probably the best conservation measure yet introduced in B.C., protecting the 4.7 million hectares of land in the agricultural reserve against creeping urban sprawl and other forms of attrition.

Cultivation of the land for crops and grazing stock necessarily changes the natural environment, but throughout history, farming has taken precedence over wildlife and will continue to do so in order that man may survive. Although farmland in B.C. is in desperately short supply, other human needs seem sometimes to dictate its sacrifice. The province's expanding population has increased the demand for hydroelectric power, and the building of more dams will inevitably mean the flooding of more valley farmland. The Site C dam of the Peace River project alone will inundate more than 3000 hectares of classified farmland, some of it the best in northern B.C. So far, with improved mechanization and farm methods and with more of the potential agricultural land being brought into production each year (12 000 hectares were added in 1980), the attrition of B.C. farmland has meant no loss of productivity. But to satisfy future food needs, what little farmland the province possesses must be surrendered only when it is absolutely necessary.

The Fisheries

Long before the coming of European man to the Pacific Northwest, the salmon resource, one of the foundations of the coast Indian culture, was vital to the peoples of B.C., and it has remained so. Today, the commercial fishery is the province's fourth most important economic activity, and salmon accounts for 75 percent of the catch.

The first settlers were astounded by the salmon's abundance — every fall the coastal rivers were literally choked with fish battling upstream to spawn. At first the fish were caught extensively for local use, but the American invention of the canning process in the 1860s made possible the export of salmon. The first commercial cannery was built in the Fraser mouth in 1867, and by the turn of the century there were 70 factories along the coast. B.C. salmon was shipped and marketed around the world. At that time it was assumed that the salmon were in such natural abundance that no harvest controls were necessary. Fishermen caught as much as the canneries could pack; because sockeye was the species best suited to canning and much in demand for its flavour and scarlet flesh, it made up 80 percent of the early packs.

Most sockeye spawn in the Fraser River drainage and their runs were already suffering from decades of overfishing when, in 1913, landslides and rock dumping from construction of the Canadian Northern Railway blocked the river at Hell's Gate. The 1913–14 runs of both sockeye and pink salmon, unable to reach their spawning grounds, thrashed to death in the pools below the blockage. Even after the passage was cleared, the Fraser salmon continued to dwindle so drastically that in 1920 an assistant commissioner of fisheries lamented: "The Fraser is fished out. Its present condition is a monumental record of man's folly and greed." The Fraser River salmon pack had shrunk from a value of $30 million to a mere $3 million. After this disaster the fishing industry turned to other rivers; by 1928 there were canneries on every major coastal inlet. But the days of plenty could not last: fish grew scarce and many canneries were forced to close. It was finally admitted that the salmon had been overfished and that controls were needed to protect the resource.

Ocean fisheries come under federal jurisdiction. In 1937 Canada and the United States set up the International Salmon Fisheries Commission to regulate and share the slowly recovering Fraser River catch. In theory, the number of fish caught was to be balanced by the number which escaped to spawn, thus ensuring a continuous yield. The two countries signed an additional agreement with Japan in 1953 to further protect the fish supply, and in 1977 Canada increased its territorial fishing boundary from 19 kilometres to 322 kilometres in order to control the catch of other foreign fishing fleets. But the continuing demise of the Pacific salmon was due not only to overfishing but also to deterioration of water quality in the rivers and blockage or disturbance of spawning grounds. Salmon are sensitive to heat and chemical changes. High temperatures in spawning waters damage eggs and young fish, and silt or logging debris covering spawning gravels reduces oxygen content. Pollution of river waters, particularly in estuaries where young fish adjust to the salinity of the sea, is also harmful.

While some prior attempts at rehabilitation of fish habitat and enhancement of fish stocks in government hatcheries took place, the most striking action began in 1977. In an effort to reverse the decline of the resource and restore the runs of salmon and sea-run trout to historical levels of abundance, a joint federal-provincial program was started. This Salmonid Enhancement Program, which had initial funding of more than $150 million for its first seven-year phase, attacked the problem along several fronts: by improving fish access to spawning grounds; by clearing rivers, building fishways and ladders (similar to those built in 1944 at Hell's Gate); by constructing artificial spawning channels where natural gravels are inaccessible or disturbed; hatching and raising fish in hatcheries; and chemically fertilizing nutrient-poor coastal lakes to increase the size and strength of the young fish (mostly sockeye).

The success of this province-wide program is gratifying, not only because of the numbers of fish it adds to the resource (in 1981 nearly 267 million smolts were released from SEP hatcheries, a number predicted to result in nearly 4 million adult spawners) but also because of the amount of public involvement — involvement which indicates concern and even a sense of responsibility on the part of the general public. More than 7000 individual volunteers — from school children to pensioners — cleared rivers of garbage and debris, operated simple hatcheries, and transplanted hatchery-raised eggs and fry to streams depleted of natural stocks. In addition, 14 hatcheries were built and operated in 1981 by community groups, 9 of them by Indian bands who, more than any of us, are aware of the full extent of the salmon loss.

It is also a most encouraging sign of the times to see industry

Mixed forest near Fort St. John. Al Harvey

co-operating in the rehabilitation of fish habitat, admittedly degraded by its own operations. In one recent instance, the estuary of the Campbell River on Vancouver Island, a log booming ground since the turn of the century, is being restored. B.C. Forest Products has chosen to sort its logs on land and to restore the river mouth — building islands and planting marshes — for fish and wildlife habitat. The Campbell is world-renowned as a sportfishing river.

It is too early to tell whether these laudatory attempts to restore the salmon's abundance will be successful; and the long-term effects of hatchery-bred fish on the wild salmon population are not known. At the moment, it seems that the fisheries are still declining. In 1913, the climax year of the Fraser sockeye's cycle, the Fraser catch totalled 55 000 tonnes. Since then the greatest years were in the mid-1950s when catches topped 20 000 tonnes, but recently the average has dropped to below 10 000 tonnes. (A viable, self-sustaining salmon resource is essential not for the economy alone but also as an indication of the health of the total environment.)

Halibut and herring, both said to be recovering from past over-harvest, are also important to the commercial fisheries. Perhaps the future strength of the industry lies in the diversity of the catch: many other types of fish, including sole and cod, are found in the Pacific, and these, along with molluscs and crustaceans, octopus and squid, are finding a ready market. Fish that live out their lives in the deep ocean are less affected by man's activities than anadromous fish and creatures of the near-shore shallows, but oil spills from coastal supertankers or oil drilling in the coastal basin could take their toll. When the land is being used to its fullest capacity for food production, man's growing population must turn to the sea and the life it sustains. Its weeds and nourishing plankton as well as its fish will be needed to feed mankind. The ocean environment, fragile despite its huge size, must be guarded.

Power

British Columbia is well endowed with a variety of energy resources, but the one most intrinsically associated with the province — and the most controversial because of environmental consequences — is hydro-electricty. The province's precipitous terrain and its affluence of fresh water provide potential hydro power in abundance, a source less finite than the fossil fuels that most countries must rely on.

The young province was quick to realize and harness the power potential of its fast-flowing rivers: at first the height differential at natural waterfalls provided sufficient supply; then small dams were needed to increase the water drop and regulate the flow for irrigation projects and year-round generation. In the 1950s the booming B.C. economy demanded more electricity, and the province pushed forward an energy program which resulted in the building of giant dams and powerhouses and the march of countless kilometres of transmission lines.

The first large project was the Kemano dam, built by the Aluminum Company of Canada to fuel its aluminum smelter at Kitimat. The waters of the Nechako River backed up, drowning a 180-kilometre chain of lovely lakes in Tweedsmuir Provincial Park, until then one of the largest protected wilderness areas in North America. In the following years, a series of mammoth dams were built by B.C. Hydro on two great rivers, the Peace and the Columbia. The Bennett Dam near Hudson's Hope impounded the Peace and Finlay rivers to create Williston Lake, now the largest freshwater body in the province. This reservoir covers 1750 square kilometres of prime agricultural land as well as forest which had been important winter range for deer, elk and moose. On the Columbia, dams at Mica Creek, Duncan and High Arrow created giant reservoirs mainly to regulate water flow and increase power generation in the United States. Under the terms of the 1964 Columbia Treaty, B.C. built the dams in return for half the extra power generated by downstream U.S. plants for 30 years, plus flood control benefits for 60 years. The province sold its share of the extra power in advance to U.S. utility companies, but when the treaty is over in the 1990s, B.C. will be free to use the extra power for itself.

In 1980 B.C. Hydro produced a plan for more megaprojects: Site C on the Peace River to be ready in 1987; Murphy Creek dam near Castlegar, 1989; dams on the Stikine-Iskut rivers, 1991, and on the Liard River, 1994. Also planned is a diversion of the Kootenay River into the Columbia at Canal Flats. These projects are of staggering size and would all result in environmental diminishment. Before they go ahead, studies will be done and public hearings held, for every dam means the loss of something — farmland, fisheries, wildlife habitat, natural beauty, forests, historical sites — and we must weigh this loss against the benefits that additional electricity will bring. Such public hearings are increasingly well attended by a variety of interest groups — an encouraging sign of citizen concern. In one case, perhaps a turning point in public sentiment, citizen interest may have had a significant impact. The planned raising of the Ross dam in Washington would submerge a good portion of the Skagit Valley near Hope. The province signed a legally binding treaty in 1967, but public outcry on both sides of the border has delayed the issue. In 1982 B.C. has offered instead to sell Seattle the electricity it needs from its hydroelectric surplus, and there is a possibility that the valley may be spared.

At present, hydroelectric power supplies only 15 percent of provincial energy consumption. Substantially more, 45 percent, comes from oil, 22 percent from natural gas, and 17 percent from the burning of wood wastes from the forest industry. (Wood wastes, including hog fuel from sawmills and black liquor from the pulp-making process, supply 55 percent of the fuel needs of forest and related industries, a good example of maximum resource use.) B.C.'s reserves of oil are skimpy and on the decline. Its annual production of 14 million barrels satisfies only one quarter of provincial needs; the rest must be imported from Alberta. With demand for oil accelerating, B.C. has a choice: to import more, or to investigate production from offshore deposits, a decision which will be acceptable only if the ocean environment can be safeguarded. Established reserves of natural gas from the Peace River sedimentary basin are extensive, an estimated 200 trillion litres (though this is only 30 years' supply at current rates of consumption) and more is likely to be found. At the moment, B.C. exports more than half its annual gas production of over 1000 billion litres. The province also has massive proven reserves of coal — about 2600 million tonnes. Though 90 percent is metallurgical, mostly exported for steel production, the remaining thermal coal could be burned to generate electricity.

Energy alternatives are being explored in B.C. These include geothermal power (the earth's own heat from hot springs), wind power, the conversion of municipal garbage to steam heat for downtown core areas, and the increased use of solar energy for residential heating. None of these is expected to have large-scale industrial potential, and with nuclear power being dismissed as too dangerous, it may well be that some of the proposed hydro projects will need to go ahead if future power demands live up to the forecasts.

Water and Air

Clean water and air are two resources generally taken for granted in British Columbia, and we are fortunate that their quality, compared to that in other regions of Canada, has remained relatively good. Water has been the most affected by the activities of man. Over the past century, industrial chemicals, pulp and paper mill effluent, mine wastes, human sewage, detergents, pesticides and fertilizers have all been dumped into rivers and sea. The noxious effects of this pollution were not anticipated, nor were they immediately diagnosed because of the dilution capabilities of water. But the problem increased as industry and population grew, and today all the major river systems, the lakes, inlets and estuaries, are tainted to a degree. Some urban beaches are so contaminated from human sewage that swimming is prohibited, and the Fraser estuary and other areas of the Strait of Georgia are now closed to shellfish harvesting.

The Fraser, where most of the province's heavy industry is located, has suffered the most from discharges of sewage, toxic wastes and heavy metals, the latter of prime concern because of their cumulative long-term effects in the estuary. The river has also been changed by

seemingly benign activities such as dyking to prevent flooding of farmland, dredging to ensure deep water passage for large ships, the filling in of marshes to create building sites, and the storing and sorting of logs.

The Fraser River system still supports the world's largest natural salmon runs, and its estuary is a vital nursery for young salmon and trout. Its foreshores and marshlands are home to Canada's greatest wintering population of waterbirds and the single most critical resting area for a million migrant birds on the Pacific flyway. As human demands on the estuary have increased, wildlife habitat has seriously diminished.

Attempts have been made over the years to clean up the river. Sewage treatment plants have been built, industrial discharges regulated by permit (and violators prosecuted), and marshes and wetlands for wildlife have been preserved. But the major stumbling block has been one of jurisdiction. No fewer than 67 units of government — local, regional, provincial and federal — control some aspect of the river, and it has been difficult in the past for decisions to be made and legislation to be enforced. In 1977 Environment Canada and the B.C. Ministry of the Environment initiated a joint comprehensive study of the Fraser estuary. Years of inventory and research plus substantial input from other government agencies, industry and the public, have resulted in a management plan that resolves the jurisdictional impasse and provides guidelines to balance economic and environmental priorities and help bring about the enhancement of the river's natural resources. This plan is an important first step towards the restitution of the Fraser as a living river. It is also significant because it shows concern on the part of all sectors of the community for the future health of the river environment, and acknowledges the trade-offs and compromises that must be made between economic growth and ecological stability in the estuary.

The Brunette River, which enters the Fraser near New Westminster, was probably the most polluted of all the Fraser tributaries. For years it was a sewer for human and industrial wastes: its streambed was a jumble of logs and garbage; its banks eroded; its water so poisoned that it could no longer support fish. Some people believed the river to be terminally impaired. But recent efforts to revive the Brunette by stopping pollution and cleaning and restoring the streambed have been extremely successful. Even fish have been reintroduced to its waters.

The Fraser's history of abuse and gradual restitution has been repeated elsewhere in B.C., particularly in the lakes of the Okanagan and the Thompson River system. Both suffer from high levels of phosphorus, a chemical that promotes the overgrowth of algae and weeds which in turn reduces oxygen content in the water. The phosphorus comes mainly from pulp mill and sewage discharges, though orchard fertilizers also contribute. To reduce phosphorus levels, more effective methods of sewage treatment and disposal are being tried, including spray irrigation in which treated sewage is used as a grassland fertilizer, and industrial wastes are gradually being cleaned. In the Okanagan, one of the few areas of B.C. where water supplies are less than generous, water is critical for orchard irrigation. Here, where a chain of lakes is vital to the tourist trade, a water management plan for the whole basin has been put into effect to improve the quality of the lakes and balance water needs for a diversity of uses.

The condition of B.C.'s lakes and rivers is still cause for concern, particularly in northern inlets where mines can legally dump toxic wastes, but the tightening of government regulations, improved technology, more industry co-operation, and public demand for cleaner water are beginning to have results. If the Brunette River can be restored, there is hope for other waters.

Air quality in B.C. is still high, even in the Lower Mainland despite the density of industry and automobile use. The prevailing westerly winds which bring rain also bring fresh supplies of clean air to keep Vancouver and most of the province relatively smog free. Acid rain is not yet a problem here because the steel mills, thermal generating plants, and other heavy industry which cause it are still largely absent. The B.C. Ministry of the Environment monitors air quality in strategic areas throughout the province, and air pollution controls are generally being tightened.

Parks and Wildlife

Perhaps the greatest of British Columbia's resources are those not measurable in dollars and which contribute only indirectly to the economy: the splendour and diversity of the landscape, the experience of wilderness, the opportunities for outdoor recreation, and the plentiful wildlife. Without them, life in B.C. would lose its zest, its sense of special favour. But man's impact on the environment has harmed these natural assets, and the damage is likely to continue. Direct impact, such as logging and mining, is not the only threat; even people enjoying the out-of-doors are having an effect.

Alpine areas in Manning and Garibaldi parks, both close to Vancouver, are already suffering from overuse. In the fragile world of alpine moss and rock and flowers, the soil is thin, and repeated footsteps, even well-meaning ones, do much damage. Wildlife is disturbed when hordes of humans tramp through its habitat; careless handling of campfires and cigarettes often causes devasting forest fires; power boats pollute lakes, and mechanized vehicles do much damage to the terrain. Man's excursions into the wilderness are having to be increasingly regulated and his freedoms curtailed in order to preserve environmental quality. Sport

Skagit Valley, Cascade Range. Fred Chapman, Photo/Graphics

fishing and hunting are controlled, power boats are banned from a growing number of lakes, and the use of recreational vehicles, particularly snowmobiles, is restricted. Camping is limited in alpine parkland, and on the meadows, hikers must keep to the trails. To some, these are unpleasant restraints on the unlimited freedom they have come to expect from the wilderness experience. Yet these restrictions are increasingly necessary.

Today, five percent of the area of B.C., a total of 4.5 million hectares, has been set aside as parkland. At the turn of the century wilderness was not considered an asset but only a hindrance to resource development, so it is remarkable that any was preserved. The first provincial parks, Strathcona (1911), Mount Robson (1913) and Garibaldi (1920) were established as revenue-producing tourist attractions similar to the national parks of the Rockies. When tourists failed to materialize, the economic worth of these wilderness areas was reappraised. Fortunately, park status was preserved, but resource development, mostly mining and logging, was permitted. When other parks were set aside, it was on a similar basis of resource availability, and consequently some of the early parks were reduced in size and their quality diminished through resource exploitation. But at least a park framework was there.

In 1965 the B.C. government defined a new category for parks, Class A, in which resource development was finally banned. It also created nature conservancies, true wilderness enclaves where people are not encouraged to go, and set up buffer-zone recreation areas around existing parks. Expansion of the parks system began in 1972 with the establishment of Class A Mount Edziza Park in the volcano lands of the northwest. Ten new Class A parks were created the following year, and three years later the nearly 700 000-hectare Spatsizi Plateau Wilderness Park was set aside. With many other smaller provincial parks, Pacific Rim National Park on Vancouver Island's west coast, the splendid Rocky Mountain parks, and the Ministry of Forests' recreation sites, trails and canoe routes throughout the province, British Columbians are well-endowed with accessible "wilderness." Yet convincing arguments for more parkland are not hard to find; a growing population and an increasing awareness of the delights of nature will bring more pressures to bear on the parks system. And if there are to be future additions, these areas would be better set aside now before resource development alters their beauty or diminishes their wildlife.

In addition to the provincial parks system, B.C. has instituted a system of ecological reserves: totally protected areas in which even fishing and camping are forbidden. Under this program, a first for Canada, B.C. has preserved samples of a diversity of natural environments: offshore islets, bogs and marshes, alpine meadows, desert, grassland, forest, hot springs, lakes — living museums of the environment for

Stream in the Rocky Mountains, near Valemount. Al Harvey

research and study. So far, more than 100 reserves have been established since the program began in 1971.

There are more than 600 species of wildlife in B.C., ranging in size from the tiny hummingbird to the giant grizzly bear and in numbers from rare to abundant. Big game is in good supply. The mountains support North America's largest populations of grizzly, cougar, wolf, mountain sheep and goat, and elsewhere moose, deer, black bear and elk are common. Over the past century man and his activities have encroached on wildlife habitat, affecting the sizes of natural populations, sometimes for the better but more often for the worse.

Deer and moose prefer open brushland where they can browse on the tender shoots of young deciduous growth. Burned-over areas — the aftermath of forest fires — provided ideal natural habitat, and interior Indians often deliberately set fire to the forest to keep game supplies near. Commercial logging had much the same effect as fires in increasing deer and moose habitat, and as the forests declined, both species proliferated, the moose dramatically. Unseen south of Prince George or west of the Rockies before the turn of the century, moose is now common east of the Coast Mountain divide as far south as the international boundary and beyond. The adaptable coyote has also benefited from man's presence because it preys on the rodents that agricultural land clearings encourage.

Other species have decreased in range and numbers and several have been designated by the provincial Ministry of the Environment as in danger of immediate extinction: the Vancouver Island marmot, the white pelican, the sea otter, the burrowing owl and the bison. The anatum peregrine falcon and the yellow badger have been classified as threatened. Wildlife decline is attributed mainly to loss of habitat, a continuing problem which the Fish and Wildlife branch is addressing in two ways: by buying and preserving parcels of land critical for wildife, and through a program of integrated land management.

The salvage of wildlife habitat began in the early 1950s, and today nearly a million hectares are under some form of provincial government control. Most of this is rangeland for deer, elk and other ungulates, but 78 000 hectares are estuary, marsh and riverbank habitat, types of environment generally in short supply and critical for fish and waterfowl. Some of the land was acquired and leased to the government by the National Second Century Fund of B.C., an independent conservation trust; other parcels were bought by the provincial Habitat Conservation Fund, donated by industry or by individuals, or transferred from other government jurisdictions. Among these preserved lands are 200 hectares of habitat for the endangered Vancouver Island marmot, given by MacMillan Bloedel; nearly 6000 hectares of grassland at the junction of the Fraser and Chilcotin rivers, winter range for one of the largest bands of California bighorn sheep in the world; and critical marshlands in the Fraser estuary.

Specific site acquisition, though in some cases vital, is not by itself sufficient to ensure the future well-being of B.C.'s wildlife heritage, according to the Ministry of the Environment. What is needed in addition is management of all crown lands, including the 70 million hectares of forest and range, for integrated multiple use, including wildlife conservation. The government's Co-ordinated Resource Management Plan and the new Forest Act are responses to this need.

Although in the past B.C. wildlife has suffered at man's hand (though never as disastrously as the sea otter, extirpated through over-hunting in the eighteenth and nineteenth centuries), the past decade has seen noticeable improvements, both in public concern and government action. Strict hunting regulations and management for sustained yield of all the species hunted for sport are major advances. Habitat preservation and enhancement are others. And B.C. wildlife is beginning to show signs of resurgence. The Vancouver Island wolf, decimated by early persecution and loss of forest habitat, has made a dramatic comeback; the sea otter has been reintroduced off the west coast of Vancouver Island and its population, though officially endangered, is reportedly stable; elk have increased in the past 10 years, particularly in the East Kootenay, and the numbers of mountain sheep and goats are constant after many years of decline. Even the Vancouver Island marmot is said to be on the increase. If current wildlife programs are continued, one of B.C.'s major natural resources may be assured a healthy future.

The past 100 years — the debit side of the ledger — have seen much abuse of B.C.'s resource heritage. We are fortunate that so much is left — the province is generally perceived to be among the last great approachable yet unspoiled wilderness areas in North America. No other region can match it in diversity of landscape, wildlife and recreational opportunities. Its unfettered space is a privilege in an overpopulated and industrialized world. As long as British Columbians continue to take pride in their land, as long as their attitudes favour conservation, there is still hope that the splendour of the province may endure.

Alders in the lower Fraser Valley. Bob Herger, Photo/Graphics

Valerian, paintbrush and anemone on Mt. Assiniboine. M.E. Schretlen, B.C. Ministry of the Environment

Some Native Species of B.C.

TREES

Alpine fir, *Abies lasiocarpa* Nutt.
Alpine larch, *Larix lyallii* Pall.
Arctic willow, *Salix arctica* Pall.
Arbutus, *Arbutus menziesii* Pursh.
Amabilis fir, *Abies amabilis* Forb.
Big-leaf maple, *Acer macrophyllum* Pursh.
Black hawthorn, *Crataegus douglasii* Lindl.
Black spruce, *Picea mariana* B.S.P.
Chokecherry, *Prunus virginiana* L.
Dogwood, *Cornus nuttallii* Audubon.
Douglas-fir, *Pseudotsuga menziesii* Franco.
Englemann spruce, *Picea engelmannii* Engelm.
Green alder, *Alnus sinuata* Rydberg.
Garry oak, *Quercus garryana* Hook.
Grand fir, *Abies grandis* Lindl.
Juniper, *Juniperus communis* Lindl.
Lodgepole pine, *Pinus contorta latifolia* Engelm.
Mountain-ash, *Sorbus sitchensis* Roemer.
Mountain hemlock, *Tsuga mertensiana* Carr.
Ponderosa pine, *Pinus ponderosa* Law.
Red alder, *Alnus rubra* Bong.
Scrub birch, *Betula glandulosa* Michx.
Shore pine, *Pinus contorta contorta* Dougl.
Sitka spruce, *Picea sitchensis* Carr.
Tamarack, *Larix laricina* K. Koch.
Trembling aspen, *Populus tremuloides* Michx.
Vine maple, *Acer circinatum* Pursh.
Western hemlock, *Tsuga heterophylla* Sarg.
Western larch, *Larix occidentalis* Nutt.
Western redcedar, *Thuja plicata* D. Don.
Western white pine, *Pinus monticola* D. Don.
Whitebark pine, *Pinus albicaulis* Engelm.
Yellowcedar, *Chamaecyparis nootkatensis* Spach.

SHRUBS

Antelope bush, *Purshia tridentata* D.C.
Bearberry, *Arctostaphylos uva-ursi* Spreng.
Bog cranberry, *Vaccinium oxycoccos* L.
Blue-berry elder, *Sambucus cerulea* Raf.
Bunchberry, *Cornus canadensis* L.
Cloudberry, *Rubus chamaemorus* L.
Copper bush, *Cladothamnus pyrolaeflorus* Bong.
Devil's club, *Oplopanox horridus* Miquel.
False azalea, *Menziesia ferruginea* Smith.
False box, *Pachistima myrsinites* Pursh.
Flowering currant, *Ribes sanguineum* Pursh.
Huckleberry, red, *Vaccinium parvifolium* Smith.
Labrador tea, *Ledum groenlandicum* Oder.
Mock-orange, *Philadelphus lewisii* Pursh.
Pink rhododendron, *Rhododendron macrophyllum* G. Don.
Poison ivy, *Rhus radicans* L.
Rabbitbrush, *Chrysothemnus nauseosus* Pall.

Red-berry elder, *Sambucus racemosa* L.
Red osier dogwood, *Cornus stolonifera* Michx.
Red raspberry, *Rubus idaeus* L.
Sagebrush, *Artemisa tridentata* Nutt.
Salal, *Gaultheria shallon* Pursh.
Salmonberry, *Rubus spectabilis* Pursh.
Saskatoon, *Amelanchier florida* Lindl.
Swamp laurel, *Kalmia polifolia* Wang.
Sumac, *Rhus glabra* L.
Trailing blackberry, *Rubus ursinus* L.
White rhododendron, *Rhododendron albiflorum* Hook.
Wormwood, *Artemisia frigida* Willd.

FLOWERS

Alpine daisy, *Erigeron peregrinus* Pursh.
Alpine forget-me-not, *Myosotis alpestris* Schmidt.
Anemone, Canadian, *Anemone drummondii* S. Wats..
Anemone, western, *Anemone occidentalis* S. Wats.
Arnica, *Arnica diversifolia* L.
Balsam-root sunflower, *Balsamorhiza sagittata* Nutt..
Bitter root, *Lewisii rediviva* Pursh.
Bleeding heart, *Dicentra uniflora* Kell.
Blue-eyed grass, *Sisyrinchium angustifolium* Miller.
Blue-eyed mary, *Collinsia parviflora* Lindl.
Brodiaea, *Triteleia grandiflora* Lindl.
Broom, *Cytisus scoparius* L..
Brown-eyed susan, *Gaillardia aristata* Pursh.
Buckwheat, *Eriogonum flavum* Nutt.
Cactus, *Opuntia fragilis* Nutt.
Camas, *Camassia quamash* Pursh.
Canada thistle, *Cirsium arvense* L.
Columbine, blue, *Aquilegia brevistyla* Hook.
Columbine, red, *Aquilegia formosa* Fisch.
Death camas, *Zygadenus venenosus* S. Wats.
Erythronium, *Erythronium oregonum* Applegate.
False Solomon's seal, *Smilacina racemosa* L.
Fireweed, *Epilobium angustifolium* L.
Flax, *Linum perenne* L.
Foam-flower, *Tiarella laciniata* Hook.
Geranium, sticky, *Geranium viscosissimum* F. & M.
Gorse, *Ulex europaeus* L.
Gumweed, *Grindelia integrifolia* D.C.
Heather, *Cassiope mertensiana* Bong.
Honeysuckle, *Lonicera* spp. L.
Indian hellebore, *Veratrum viride* Ait.
Indian paintbrush, *Castilleja miniata* Dougl.
Indian pipe, *Monotropa uniflora* L.
Lungwort, *Mertensia oblongifolia* Nutt.
Lupine, *Lupinus arcticus* S. Wats.
Lupine, silky, *Lupinus sericeus* Pursh.

Mariposa lily, *Calochortus macrocarpus* Dougl.
Meadow spirea, *Spiraea betulifolia* Pall.
Milkweed, *Asclepius speciosa* Torr.
Mimulus, *Mimulus guttatus* D.C.
Moss campion, *Silene acaulis* L.
Mountain heath, *Phyllodoce empetriformis* Smith.
Oregon fairy bells, *Disporum hookeri* Torrey.
Oxalis, *Oxalis oregana* Nutt.
Phacelia, *Phacelia linearis* Pursh.
Phlox, creeping, *Phlox diffusa* Benth.
Phlox, long-leaved, *Phlox longifolia* Nutt.
Prickly rose, *Rosa nutkana hispida* Presl.
Purple aster, *Aster conspicuus* Lindl.
Sagebrush buttercup, *Ranunculus glaberrimus* Hook.
Satin flower, *Sisyrinchium douglasii* Dietr.
Scarlet gilia, *Gilia aggregata* Pursh.
Sea blush, *Plectritis congesta* Lindl.
Shooting star, *Dodecatheon pulchellum* Raf.
Skunk cabbage, *Lysichitum americanum* Hult. & St. J.
Snow-lily, *Erythronium grandiflorum* Pursh.
Soopolallie, *Shepherdia canadensis* L.
Starflower, *Trientalis latifolia* Hook.
Sundew, *Drosera rotundifolia* Huds.
Thrift, *Armeria maritima* Mill.
Tigerlily, *Lilium columbianum* Hanson.
Trillium, *Trillium ovatum* Pursh.
Twinflower, *Linnaea borealis* Gronov.
Yellow bell, *Fritillaria pudica* Pursh.
Yellow paintbrush, *Castilleja levisecta* Greemn.
Vanilla leaf, *Achlys triphylla* Smith.
Valerian, *Valeriana dioica* L.
Vetch, *Vica sativa* L.
Violet, blue, *Viola adunca* Smith.
Violet, yellow, *Viola glabella* Nutt.
Wild lily-of-the-valley, *Maianthemum canadense* Desf.
Wild ginger, *Asarum caudatum* Lindl.
Wood lily, *Lilium philadelphicum* L.

MAMMALS

Badger, *Taxidea taxus*
Beaver, *Castor canadensis*
Bighorn sheep, *Ovis canadensis*
Black bear, *Ursus americanus*
Black-tailed deer (coast), *Odocoileus hemionus columbianus*
Caribou, *Rangifer tarandus*
Cottontail, *Sylvilagus nuttalli*
Cougar, *Felis concolor*
Coyote, *Canis latrans*
Dall porpoise, *Phocoenoides dalli dalli*
Dall sheep, *Ovis dalli*
Douglas squirrel, *Tamiasciurus douglasii*
Elk, Rocky Mountain, *Cervus elaphus nelsoni*

Elk, Roosevelt, *Cervus elaphus roosevelti*
Fisher, *Martes pennanti*
Flying squirrel, *Glaucomys sabrinus*
Grizzly bear, *Ursus horribilis*
Harbour porpoise, *Phocoena phocoena*
Harbour (hair) seal, *Phoca vitulina*
Harvest mouse, *Reithrodontomys megalotis*
Hoary marmot, *Marmota caligata*
Humpback whale, *Megaptera novaeangliae*
Jumping mouse, *Zapus trinotatus*
Killer whale, *Orcinus orca*
Lynx, *Felis lynx*
Marten, *Martes americana*
Mink, *Mustela vison*
Moose, *Alces alces*
Mountain goat, *Oreamnos americanus*
Mule deer, *Odocoileus hemionus hemionus*
Muskrat, *Ondatra zibethicus*
Northwestern chipmunk, *Eutamias amoenus*
Pika, *Ochotona princeps*
Pocket gopher, *Thomomys talpoides*
Pocket mouse, *Perognathus parvus*
Porcupine, *Erethizon dorsatum*
Raccoon, *Procyon lotor*
Red fox, *Vulpes vulpes*
Red squirrel, *Tamiasciurus hudsonicus*
River otter, *Lutra canadensis*
Steller's sea-lion, *Eumetopias jubata*
Stone sheep, *Ovis dalli stonei*
Timber wolf, *Canis lupus*
Weasel, *Mustela frenata*
White-tailed deer, *Odocoileus virginianus*
White-tailed jackrabbit, *Lepus townsendii*
Wolverine, *Gulo gulo*
Woodchuck, *Marmota monax*
Yellow-bellied marmot, *Marmota flaviventris*

BIRDS

Ancient murrelet, *Synthliboramphum antiquus*
Bald eagle, *Haliaeetus leucocephalus*
Band-tailed pigeon, *Columba fasciata*
Belted kingfisher, *Megaceryle alcyon*
Black-backed three-toed woodpecker, *Picoides arcticus*
Black brant, *Branta nigricans*
Black oystercatcher, *Haematopus bachmani*
Black tern, *Chlidonias niger*
Black turnstone, *Arenaria melanocephala*
Blue grouse, *Dendragapus obscurus*
Blue jay (eastern), *Cyanocitta cristata*
Blue-winged teal, *Anas discors*
Bobolink, *Dolichonyx oryzivorus*
Bohemian waxwing, *Bombycilla garrulus*
Bonaparte's gull, *Larus philadelphia*
Boreal chickadee, *Parus hudsonicus*
Boreal owl, *Aegolius funereus*
Brandt's cormorant, *Phalacrocorax penicillatus*
Brewer's sparrow, *Spizella breweri*
Bufflehead, *Bucephala albeola*
Bushtit, *Psaltriparus minimus*

Calliope hummingbird, *Stellula calliope*
California quail, *Lophortyx californicus*
Canada goose, *Branta canadensis*
Canvasback duck, *Aythya valisineria*
Cassin's auklet, *Ptychoramphus aleutica*
Chestnut-backed chickadee, *Parus rufescens*
Chukar, *Alectoris graeca*
Cinnamon teal, *Anas cyanoptera*
Clark's nutcracker, *Nucifraga columbiana*
Coot, *Fulica americana*
Dowitcher, long-billed, *Limnodromus scolopaceus*
Downy woodpecker, *Picoides pubescens*
Dunlin, *Erolia alpina*
Eastern kingbird, *Tyrannus tyrannus*
Fork-tailed storm petrel, *Oceanodroma furcata*
Glaucous-winged gull, *Larus glaucescens*
Golden-crowned kinglet, *Regulus satrapa*
Golden eagle, *Aquila chrysaetos*
Goldeneye duck, Barrow's, *Bucephala islandica*
Goldeneye duck, common, *Bucephala clangula*
Gray-crowned rosy finch, *Leucosticte tephrocotis*
Gray partridge, *Perdix perdix*
Great blue heron, *Ardea herodias*
Great northern diver (see Loon, common)
Green heron, *Butorides striatus*
Hairy woodpecker, *Picoides villosus*
Horned lark, *Eremophila alpestris*
Gray jay (Canada jay), *Perisoreus canadensis*
Kestrel, American, *Falco sparverius*
Lazuli bunting, *Passerina amoena*
Leach's storm petrel, *Oceanodroma leucorhoa*
Lewis's woodpecker, *Melanerpes lewis*
Long-billed curlew, *Numenius americanus*
Loon, common, *Gavia immer*
Magnolia warbler, *Dendroica magnolia*
Magpie, *Pica pica*
Mallard, *Anas platyrhynchos*
Meadowlark, western, *Sturnella neglecta*
Mountain bluebird, *Sialia currucoides*
Mourning dove, *Zenaidura macroura*
Murre, common, *Uria aalge*
Nighthawk, *Chordeiles minor*
Northwestern crow, *Corvus caurinus*
Peregrine falcon, *Falco peregrinus*
Phalarope, Wilson's, *Steganopus tricolor*
Pileated woodpecker, *Dryocopus pileatus*
Poorwill, *Phalaenoptilus nuttallii*
Redhead, *Aythya americana*
Redstart, *Setophaga ruticilla*
Red-tailed hawk, *Buteo jamaicensis*
Red-winged blackbird, *Agelaius phoeniceus*
Rhinoceros auklet, *Cerorhinca monocerata*
Ring-necked pheasant, *Phasianus colchicus*
Robin, *Turdus migratorius*
Rock wren, *Salpinctes obsoletus*
Ruddy duck, *Oxyura jamaicensis*
Rufous hummingbird, *Selasphorus rufus*

Sanderling, *Crocethia alba*
Sandhill crane, *Grus canadensis*
Sandpiper, western, *Calidris mauri*
Say's phoebe, *Sayornis saya*
Shoveller duck, *Spatula clypeata*
Skylark, *Alauda arvensis*
Snowy owl, *Nyctea scandiaca*
Spruce grouse, *Canachites canadensis*
Steller's jay, *Cyanocitta stelleri*
Surfbird, *Aphriza virgata*
Swainson's thrush, *Hylocichla ustulata*
Tufted puffin, *Lunda cirrhata*
Turkey vulture, *Cathartes aura*
Varied thrush, *Ixoreus naevius*
Water pipit, *Anthus spinoletta*
Western kingbird, *Tyrannus verticalis*
Western sandpiper, *Ereunetes mauri*
Western tanager, *Piranga ludoviciana*
White-crowned sparrow, *Zonotrichia albicollis*
White-headed woodpecker, *Picoides albolarvatus*
White pelican, *Pelecanus erythrorhynches*
White-tailed ptarmigan, *Lagopus leucurus*
White-throated swift, *Aeronautes saxatalis*
Wigeon, American, *Anas americana*
Willow ptarmigan, *Lagopus lagopus*
Winter wren, *Troglodytes troglodytes*
Wood duck, *Aix sponsa*
Yellow-bellied sapsucker, *Sphyrapicus varius*
Yellow-breasted chat, *Icteria virens*
Yellow-headed blackbird, *Xanthocephalus xanthocephalus*
Yellowlegs, *Totanus flavipes*
Yellowthroat, *Geothlypis trichas*

FISH

Arctic grayling, *Thymallus arcticus*
Brill, *Eopsetta jordani*
Cutthroat trout, *Salmo clarki*
Dolly Varden, *Salvelinus malma*
Dover sole, *Microstomus pacificus*
Halibut, *Hippoglossus hippoglossus*
Herring, *Clupa herengus pallasi*
Kokanee (see Salmon, sockeye)
Lake trout, *Salvelinus namaycush*
Lemon sole, *Parophrys vetulus*
Mountain whitefish, *Prosopium williamsoni*
Northern pike, *Esox lucius*
Oolichan, *Thaleichthys pacificus*
Rainbow trout, *Salmo gairdneri*
Red snapper, *Sebastes ruberrimus*
Rock sole, *Lepidopsetta bilineata*
Salmon, chinook, *Oncorhynchus tshawytscha*
Salmon, chum, *O. keta*
Salmon, coho, *O. kisutch*
Salmon, pink, *O. gorbuscha*
Salmon, sockeye, *O. nerka*
Steelhead trout, *Salmo gairdneri*
Turbot (Arrowtooth flounder), *Atheresthes stomias*
Walleye, *Stizostedion vitreum vitreum*
White sturgeon, *Acipenser transmontanus*

Selected Bibliography

Many books, government publications and reports, maps and pamphlets were used in research for this book. Here is a list of those found to be most useful, either for general background or for specific facts.

GEOLOGY

Baird, David M. *A Guide to Geology for Visitors in Canada's National Parks.* Toronto: MacMillan, 1974.

Holland, Stuart S. *Landforms of British Columbia: a Physiographic Outline.* Victoria British Columbia Department of Mines and Petroleum Resources, Queen's Printer, 1976.

Kendrew, W.G., and Kerr, D. *The Climate of British Columbia and the Yukon.* Ottawa: Queen's Printer, 1955.

FLORA AND FAUNA

Bodsworth, Fred. *The Pacific Coast: Illustrated Natural History of Canada.* Toronto: Natural Science of Canada, 1970.

Carl, George Clifford. *Guide to Marine Life of British Columbia.* Victoria: Queen's Printer, 1970.

Clark, Lewis J. *Wild Flowers of the Pacific Northwest.* Sidney, B.C. Gray's, 1976.

Hitchcock, C. Leo, and Conquist, Arthur. *Vascular Plants of the Pacific Northwest.* Vols. 1-5. Washington: University of Washington Press, 1961.

Keeler, Harriet L. *Our Northern Shrubs, and How to Identify Them.* New York: Dover, 1969.

Little, Elbert L., and Viereck, Leslie A. *Alaska Trees and Shrubs.* Washington D.C.: U.S. Department of Agriculture, Forest Service, 1972.

Peattie, Donald C. *Natural History of Western Trees.* Boston: Houghton Mifflin, 1953.

Welsh, Stanley J. *Anderson's Flora of Alaska and Adjacent Parts of Canada.* Provo, Utah: Brigham Young University Press, 1974.

BIRDS, FISH AND MAMMALS

Banfield, A.W.F. *The Mammals of Canada.* Toronto: University of Toronto Press, 1974.

Cowan, Ian McTaggart, and Guiguet, Charles J. *The Mammals of British Columbia.* Victoria: Queen's Printer, 1965.

Edwards, R. Yorke. *The Mountain Barrier: Illustrated Natural History of Canada.* Toronto: Natural Science of Canada, 1972.

Peterson, Roger T. *Field Guide to Western Birds.* Boston: Houghton, Mifflin, 1971.

Snively, Gloria Jean. *Exploring the Seashore: a Guide to Shorebirds, and Intertidal Plants and Animals of British Columbia.* Vancouver: Soules, 1978.

Whitaker, John O., Jr. *The Audubon Society Field Guide to North American Mammals.* New York: Alfred A. Knopf, 1980.

Wooding, Frederick H. *Book of Canadian Fishes.* Toronto: McGraw-Hill Ryerson, 1972.

HISTORY AND RESOURCES

Akrigg, G.P.V., and Akrigg, Helen B. *British Columbia Chronicle, 1778-1846: Adventurers by Sea and Land.* Vancouver: Discovery Press, 1975.

————. *British Columbia Chronicle, 1847-1871: Gold and Colonists. Vancouver: Discovery Press, 1977.*

Berton, Pierre. *The Last Spike, The Great Railway 1881-1885.* Toronto: McClelland and Stewart, 1971.

British Columbia. *Inventory of Natural Resources of British Columbia.* Victoria: Queen's Printer, 1964.

Farley, A.L. *Atlas of British Columbia: People, Environment, and Resource Use.* Vancouver: University of British Columbia Press, 1979.

Fisher, Robin. *Contact and Conflict: Indian-European Relations in British Columbia 1774-1896.* Vancouver: University of British Columbia Press, 1977.

Haig-Brown, Roderick. *The Living Land: an Account of the Natural Resources of British Columbia.* Toronto: MacMillan, 1961.

McDonald, Robert A.J. "Vancouver, Victoria, and the Economic Development of British Columbia." In *British Columbia: Historical Readings,* edited by W. Peter Ward and Robert A.J. McDonald. Vancouver: Douglas and McIntyre, 1981.

Ormsby, Margaret. *British Columbia: A History.* Toronto: MacMillan, 1971.

Oxford Atlas of the United States and Canada. London: Oxford University Press, 1967.

Ralston, Keith. "Patterns of Trade and Investment on the Pacific Coast, 1867-1892: The Case of the British Columbia Salmon Canning Industry." In *British Columbia: Historical Readings,* edited by W. Peter Ward and Robert A.J. McDonald. Vancouver: Douglas & McIntyre, 1981.

Reid, David J. "Company Mergers in the Fraser River Salmon Canning Industry, 1885-1902." In *British Columbia: Historical Readings,* edited by W. Peter Ward and Robert A.J. McDonald. Vancouver: Douglas & McIntyre, 1981.

Robinson, J. Lewis., ed. *British Columbia.* Toronto: University of Toronto Press, 1972.

————, and Hardwick, Walter G. *British Columbia: One Hundred Years of Geographical Change.* Vancouver: Talonbooks: 1973.

Siemens, Alfred H. *The Lower Fraser Valley: Evolution of a Cultural Landscape.* Vancouver: Tantalus Research, 1978.

Index of Photographers

Fred Chapman, Photo/Graphics 5, 8, 71, 150
Daniel Conrad 10, 24, 30, 34-5, 37, 48, 57, 66, 75, 90, 96, 111, 130, 138, 146-7
Pierre Dow, Vancouver Aquarium 82
John Ford 92
Ed Gifford, Photo/Graphics 16, 100
Al Harvey 1, 2, 6, 52, 126, 142, 152

Bob Herger, Photo/Graphics 23, 72, 78, 112, 113, 155
Robert Keziere 103, 132
J.A. Kraulis, Photo/Graphics 12, 40, 46, 50, 60, 118, 128
Gunter Marx, Photo/Graphics 58, 73, 94
Duncan McDougall, Photo/Graphics 80, 104

Pat Morrow, Photo/Graphics 26, 44, 61, 65, 76, 121, 122, 136
M.E. Schretlen, B.C. Ministry of the Environment 156
Jürgen Vogt, Photo/Graphics 88
Richard Wright, Photo/Graphics 20, 28, 108-9, 114

British Columbia: This Favoured Land was designed by Robert Bringhurst Ltd., Vancouver, photoset by Vancouver Typesetting Co. Ltd., and printed and bound by D.W. Friesen & Sons, with colour separations by Jack Berger Ltd.

The text face is ITC Garamond, designed in 1974 by Tony Stan. It is a modern variation on a font cut by Jean Jannon in 1615 at Sedan. Jannon's letters were long misidentified as the work of Claude Garamont, later called Garamond, the brilliant designer and publisher who died penniless in Paris in 1561. The Jannon fonts and their derivatives are still, therefore, by force of custom, generally known under a form of Garamont's name.